DISCIPLINE THAT LASTS A LIFETIME

Discipline
That Lasts a Lifetime

The Best Gift You Can Give Your Kids

Dr. Ray Guarendi

PUBLISHED BY ST. ANTHONY MESSENGER PRESS
CINCINNATI, OHIO

Some material that appears in this book has been previously published in Dr. Ray Guarendi's multimedia presentation entitled *You're a Better Parent Than You Think!*

Cover design: UDG DesignWorks, Sisters, Oregon

Library of Congress Cataloging-in-Publication Data

Guarendi, Raymond N.
  Discipline that lasts a lifetime : the best gift you can give your
kids / Raymond N. Guarendi.
     p. cm.
  ISBN 1-56955-368-8 (alk. paper)
  1. Discipline of children. 2. Child rearing. I. Title.
  HQ770.4.G82 2002
  649'.64–dc21

                                                    2002155701

ISBN 1-56955-368-8

Published by Servant Books, an imprint of St. Anthony Messenger Press
28 W. Liberty St.
Cincinnati, OH 45202
www.AmericanCatholic.org

Printed in the United States of America
Printed on acid-free paper

05 06 10 9 8 7 6 5 4

Dedication

To Randi, my wife and soul mate.
To Andrew, Hannah, Jonathan, Joanna, Sarah, Samuel,
James, Mary, Peter, and Elizabeth, gifts of God.

Acknowledgments

To paraphrase the bard, "No book is an island." Many thanks are due to many people in many places. To Carol Hoppel, who typed for me and supported me from the beginning. To Sheila McLouth and Abby Kerr, who added their typing and grammatical commentary. And to my daughter, Hannah, who, at age fourteen, types and keeps her dad's spaciness from spinning out of control.

To all the publications—from the monthly locals to the major nationals—who believed the columns had something to say, and still think so.

To Bert Ghezzi at Servant Publications, who asked me what I had going in the way of books, and who pushed me to keep it going.

To Paul Thigpen, my editor, who polished words and pulled together many separate threads.

To my children, for their unending stream of material and examples. They've made me a better writer and much better father.

Contents

A Word From the Author

Discipline—it's a word that once had a pretty good reputation. Parents instinctively knew that discipline was something kids needed. It was good for them. It taught them the basics of living: character, morals, responsibility, respect.

But in the last generation or two, discipline has taken a spanking. Experts proclaim that really savvy parents shouldn't have to discipline much. They can talk and reason children into cooperating instead. The media bombard parents with all the latest theories on psychological correctness. And the culture relentlessly echoes the attitude that words such as "authority," "limits," and "control" are old-fashioned concepts we need to throw off.

No matter what trendy notions permeate parenting today, reality always wins. Discipline still is critical to raising moral people. It still is a loving, durable gift that lasts a lifetime. And it still is something parents instinctively know is good for their children.

What do I mean by "discipline"? Poll a hundred people—parents or experts—and you'll likely get a hundred varying definitions of the word. Some might say the only good discipline is an old-fashioned spanking. Others would define discipline as teaching. The former is too narrow for our purposes, and the latter is too broad, as much of parenting teaches even when no discipline is involved.

As used in the questions to come, "discipline" will be defined in a pretty straightforward, common sense manner: to put limits and expectations upon a child's behavior, backed by consequences when necessary in order to socialize and build character.

Indeed, no area of child rearing causes more day-to-day uncertainty, guilt, and frustration than discipline. We may find ourselves asking, Are my expectations too high? Am I too strict? Too lax? When should I discipline? Where? How much? What if I'm wrong? How can I get my kids to listen? Is their behavior normal?

Why am I so sure that discipline is a top concern among parents today? The sheer numbers of those who want to talk about it. The great majority of parents who attend my seminars are seeking discipline guidance.

Most of my counseling clients come to me out of frustration in this area. They are not enjoying their kids as they had hoped because the kids' behavior is so unruly. Indeed, 90 percent of what parents ask me concerns discipline. They want direction, peace, and a better relationship with their children.

This book is a collection of the most common questions I receive from parents. Originally these articles appeared as columns for publication throughout the country. You'll probably notice some common themes running through my answers.

First, you know what's best for your child.

Second, authority is not a bad word.

Third, discipline, by and large, is not complicated. Good ideas for administering discipline are straightforward and easy for you to use. Similar techniques can work for a wide range of problems.

Finally, and most importantly, parenthood is God-designed to be enjoyed. We're all in this together. We share the same worries and frustrations. So let's lighten up, laugh more, and love our children enough to do what's best for them—and for us, too.

Ray Guarendi

ONE

Discipline: Love in Action

Discipline forms the very foundation of morals and character. It is teaching done at the hands of a parent, the most loving, gentle hands most children will ever learn from. Discipline now, and your children won't be disciplined later—by the world, by people who don't love them with a fraction of your love. Discipline is a most durable form of love. It lasts a lifetime.

Why Discipline?

Dear Dr. Ray,

I know that discipline is a necessary part of parenting, but I feel guilty when I discipline. It makes me feel mean.

Too Soft?

A prime motive for discipline is this: You are the most kind, gentle teacher that your children will ever have. Never again will they be taught how to get along in life by anyone who has so much love for them.

If you don't discipline now, for whatever reason—because you feel guilty or too strict, or are afraid of doing something "wrong," or you think it's just easier to let them go—then who will ultimately discipline your children? The world. And the world is not a kind or gentle place to learn lessons.

If a parent doesn't teach qualities such as self-control, respect for others, consideration, and ability to follow rules, then the teaching task is thrust upon others: a teacher, employer, landlord, army sergeant, police officer, judge. Who of these has the emotional attachment to your child that you do? Who will forgive and forget as many times as you will?

No matter how mean you might think you are for disciplining, you are a whole lot less mean than life itself.

When a child is five, or eight, or twelve years old and talks mean, what do you do? Maybe put him in a chair, or swat his bottom, or send him to his room, or fine him fifty cents, or make him write a two-hundred-word apology. But when he's twenty-five and talks mean, what happens? He could get beat up, or fired, or arrested. He could have to sleep on the couch!

The stakes get higher as we get older. No matter how mean you might think you are for disciplining, you are a whole lot less mean than life itself. Life puts consequences on behavior solely on the basis of how we act. It seldom takes into consideration mitigating factors such as, "Oh, she's cranky because she's tired" or "What do you expect from a middle child?"

Try telling your bosses sometime after you've verbally unloaded on them, "I'm sorry. I went to bed late last night and woke up crabby, with a headache, no less. On top of that, I still don't think I'm fully over my birth trauma." I'm sure they'll just have a good laugh and make allowances!

Parents make allowances. Because we love our children without limits, we see mitigating circumstances, sometimes even when there are none. That's the beauty of parenthood.

It's what makes our discipline have heart, our lessons come with soft landings.

All the more critical, then, that we refuse to surrender our privilege—no, our duty—to discipline. We alone are uniquely suited to teach little humans when it's easiest on them and the lessons are most durable.

A mother once told me, "I think the worst thing I could do to my son would be to allow him to be unlikable." In the short term, undisciplined children aim most of their unlikableness at their parents, who suffer the brunt of their children's demands and unruliness. In the long term, however, the undisciplined children themselves suffer most. Others quickly tire of their difficult behavior and begin to avoid them. Long after Mom and Dad have left the scene, they are left to learn on their own how to relate maturely to others.

A critical distinction must be made between the false notion, on the one hand, that discipline in and of itself is mean, and the reality, on the other, of truly mean discipline. Certainly we can be mean as we discipline. We can verbally pummel, demean, and fling all kinds of unnecessary and hurtful words and emotions. By virtue of our human weakness, all parents are prone to some mean discipline. Good parents work hard for years to reduce its presence.

Yet setting firm limits and holding children accountable for their actions is not mean at all. It is love in action. It is love that is hard for children to comprehend. Nonetheless, it is love that will endure long beyond our lifetimes in the character of the next generation we leave behind on this earth.

The Will to Discipline

Dear Dr. Ray,

I know discipline is necessary and healthy, but it's hard for me to do. How can I discipline my son less without overlooking or tolerating misbehavior?

Walking Softly

Get a stopwatch. Observe your son for one hour. Start the watch when he starts to misbehave. Stop it when he stops. Then tally the behaving and the misbehaving.

Most parents would be surprised at the score. The good times almost always outweigh the bad. In fact, the rowdiest of kids usually behave all right 90 percent of the time or better. But the reverse may seem to be true because the bad times are much more memorable.

Here's my point. It's easy—it's human nature—to overlook good times and places to encourage and praise a child. Most of us don't mean to. We're tired, or preoccupied, or disciplining another child. Still, a basic law of discipline is this: The more we notice nice behavior, the less we'll see its counterpart.

Certainly I'm not implying that you should shadow your son and spew a steady stream of affection, praise, and positive strokes. That's unrealistic, and most likely too much sugar for him to handle. There is no parent, however, who can't improve at quietly encouraging the stuff we personally view as important.

That said, in my experience, loving parents typically manage to give a good amount of childrearing positives. Further, no matter how good you get at noticing the good, you'll never come close to eliminating the need for discipline. That is an inescapable parenting fact of life. There are ways, though, to reduce the amount of discipline necessary.

First and foremost, discipline more, and you'll have to discipline less. That may sound at first like nonsense, so let me say it again: Discipline more, and you'll have to discipline less.

Put another way, we can say that the more ready and willing you are to discipline calmly and firmly the instant the situation calls for it, the less often you will need to discipline over time. You will be predictable. Your son will have few doubts about your expectations and even fewer doubts that in short order you will back them up with consequences. You will not allow twenty-eight minutes of arguing, negotiating, cajoling, and threatening to persist until, finally hitting your limit, you discipline. You will discipline at the beginning of trouble instead of at the end.

Put simply, the will to discipline makes the act of discipline less necessary.

"But if I send him to his room the instant his tone of voice gets disrespectful, I'll never see him." At first, maybe. But he's not dumb. Kids often can read grown-ups better than we can read ourselves. The more sure your son is that you'll do what you say, and *now*, the less he'll push you to do it. Put simply, the will to discipline makes the act of discipline less necessary.

Think of a mom or dad you would consider a good disciplinarian. Did you ever notice how seldom they actually discipline? They don't have to. They established their rules and expectations early and clearly, so they now spend less and less time reestablishing them.

19

A colleague once gave me this analogy: Good discipline is like putting money in the bank. Put in a healthy amount early, and you can live off the interest later. Be willing to praise more. Be willing to discipline more. The need for discipline will drop. The opportunities to praise will rise.

Change of Life

Dear Dr. Ray,

My children are ages twelve and eight. I realize now that I have not disciplined them well. When is it too late to change?

Tardy

Are you asking about changing *you* or changing *them*? It's too late to change *you* on the day you leave this earth. It's pretty much too late to change *them* on the day they move away from your home. That said, it does get harder to change all of you the longer you stay the way you are. If you intend to change anybody, it's best to start right now. Time will only make change harder for everyone.

If a youngster is not maturing well, most moms and dads realize it at some point in their parenthood. And some, like you, resolve to change things. But they are nagged by the worry that they've lost too much time. They've gone in the wrong direction too long. The die is cast.

The die may have been cast. But that doesn't mean you can't pick it up and roll again. First, some kids have temperaments that make poorly raising them hard to do. They are naturally easygoing, or mature, or pleasant, or cooperative, and while weak discipline over time can make any kid tougher to raise, the easy kids are harder to make difficult and easier to make undifficult.

If you intend to change anybody, it's best to start right now. Time will only make change harder for everyone.

Second, even though reshaping a child's character may take lots of effort, it is infinitely important to do so. So the task must always be attempted, no matter how late a parent thinks it might be. Many are the adults who have dramatically changed the course of their moral lives in the fourth, fifth, even sixth decade of life. Surely most children are more malleable than grown-ups, especially if there's a loving grown-up nearby determined to "help" them change.

Third, the longer a behavior has been forming roots, the longer it will most likely take to correct. For instance, imagine that your twelve-year-old daughter is disrespectfully argumentative. (Many parents of preteens need little imagination to picture this scenario.) So you decide to levy fifteen minutes of forced chore-labor for each bout of mouthiness.

Within weeks, even days, you should notice much better mouth control. But that won't necessarily bring about routinely pleasant interchanges. The arguments may be replaced by surly silence. That's OK. The first step towards character change has begun. You must stop the bad before the good has someplace to grow.

Fourth, and related to the above, behavior changes much more quickly than attitude. Your youngster may tone down her disrespect by 80 percent the first month because she is tired of being a chore serf, but that doesn't mean she'll inwardly respect you any more than she did last month. Remain resolute anyway. Outer change will slowly lead to inner change, if you persevere.

Here is a rough time line: One month of discipline per one year of misbehavior. In other words, for every year that a problem has been growing, stick with your new discipline for one month. If your twelve-year-old has been mouthy since age four, then use your chore-serf approach for at least eight months. If by then, you've seen little progress, reassess.

An ever-present temptation in discipline is to bounce from tactic to tactic, hoping to hit the psychological lotto, and in one brilliant stroke to reverse years of wrong way momentum. Such pinball parenting leads not only to frustration, but ultimately to the false conclusion that indeed you did wait too long and that your child is incorrigibly beyond your discipline reach.

One last point. Discipline success is not measured solely by results. Discipline also involves teaching a lesson. At one level, your discipline works instantly. It tells your sons: If you do A, I do B. The lesson is immediate, but children, like all humans, learn ever so slowly to apply the lesson to life.

Reversing Directions

Dear Dr. Ray,

Having realized that I've been a weak disciplinarian for years, should I change all at once or gradually? And how will this affect my children (ages four, seven, and eight)?

Coming to Senses

Change all at once. That's the best way. Alas, even in so doing, you will only change gradually. Though you may try with all your might, it's nearly impossible to change quickly and fully.

Your parenting style and habits have been gaining momentum for a long time. Suddenly slamming on the brakes and reversing engines won't result in an immediate 180-degree turnabout. Most likely you'll skid for a while, inch to a halt, then slowly reverse directions.

Turning around a large ship in the ocean takes up to twelve miles. And that's a ship without kids. You're not the size of a ship, but you're far more complex. Altering ship course is child's play compared to altering parenting course.

Nevertheless, you need to begin changing your ways right now and with full speed ahead. First, the longer you delay, the more time bad habits will have to harden further. Breaking bad habits a little at a time is like trying to quit smoking a little at a time. You're struggling to conquer the same behavior in which you keep indulging.

Second, changing gradually leads to changing erratically. Let's say you prioritize your list of trouble. This month you'll tackle the majors: backtalk, defiance, and sibling quibbling. Next month you'll move on to bedtime bad times, meal melees, and toy trash. What if you're still getting resistance in the big three at the end of the month? Do you allot another month, thus still ignoring the minor issues?

And when is a problem conquered? At 50 percent less? Seventy-five percent? In fact, most misbehavior never completely goes away. So if you wait until one problem is all gone, you'll never move on to any others.

Third, the faces of misconduct overlap. For example, backtalk and defiance may be intertwined with bedtime bad times. Sibling quibbling can lead to toy trash, and vice versa. You can't deal effectively with one without simultaneously dealing with the others.

One of the greater human blessings is self-awareness. Once we realize we're heading in the wrong direction, we can exert all our will to change course, if we so choose.

Fourth, bad stuff needs to be stopped now. The instant you sense you're drinking spoiled milk, do you slow your rate of swallowing, or spit it out? If your children were doing something seriously harmful, would you allow them three months to give it up? One of the greater human blessings is self-awareness. Once we realize we're heading in the wrong direction, we can exert all our will to change course, if we so choose.

So how will your kids react to the new you? They'll be shell-shocked. Who is this stranger? What kind of junk has he or she been reading? How long will this last until we get back to normal?

Kids generally don't realize what is good for them. So they resist it. That's all right. Shortly they'll come to accept that this stronger parent is here to stay and will only get stronger with time. And gradually they'll change, too. Into more mature human beings who'll learn to appreciate the way things have changed.

Discipline Is Good for the Nerves

Dear Dr. Ray,

My son (age eleven) actually seems more calm, even content, since his father and I realized we need to tighten up our discipline. Do most children want more discipline?

Surprised

In the short term, no. In the long term, yes. Standard wisdom (now there's an oxymoron) says that children down deep truly desire limits, the security of knowing what parents expect, where the line is, and what will happen if it's crossed. I agree with this, sort of.

What eleven-year-old son says to a mother, "Oh, thank you, Mother. I love it when you punish me. Your strict rules and high standards are something that I just can't resist throwing into my friends' faces to make them jealous. And you know that three-hundred-word essay on respect I have to do because I talked mean? Is it OK with you if I make it five hundred? I want this lesson to stick. Love ya."

When discipline is staring children in the face, it is not something they want, down deep or otherwise. Yet good often comes from the things kids, even adults, resist most. No, children don't like discipline. But yes, they will like the peace that will come to them and their family in the short term, and the quality that will develop in their character in the long term.

How many parents have treasured the letter from college saying, "Dear Mom and Dad, Thank you for being the parents you were. I see now how kids can act when they've had parents who give them too much and let them get away with too much ..." I wonder whether parents have to fight the urge to write back, "Thanks for noticing. But why did it take you almost twenty years and my spending $17,000 a year on your education before you realized how good a parent I really was?"

Sometimes after only a few months of learning to be stronger, parents will tell me things like this: "He seems so much more pleasant since we got more firm and consistent. I thought he would react the other way." "I can't believe I'm living with the same child. Our whole family is happier." "She told me she loved me three times last week; I think that's a record for this year."

A parent who finally and firmly takes charge soothes a child's soul. A grown-up is running the family, the way God intended it.

While kids initially may resist stronger discipline, with time they become more amenable to it. Both their demeanor and their mood settle. The explanation is pretty straightforward.

Weak discipline invites relentless challenge, causing ill will for all. Resolute discipline, on the other, lays down a stable line. When consequences are clear and sure, kids learn the terms. They cease the battle, and accept what is. Put simply, better discipline makes for a better relationship.

Draw an adult parallel. Imagine that every day at work, several times a day, you and your boss disagree and verbally assault each other over your job responsibilities. Further, your boss doesn't use legitimate company rules and authority to deal with you. Instead, you are nagged, badgered, and threatened, all in an escalating, emotional pitch.

In that situation, how long would it take for you to want to quit, to get an ulcer, or to ask your doctor for spray valium? You'd get progressively more agitated and discontent.

A parent who finally and firmly takes charge—not with more words and volume, but with real authority, and with expectations backed by action—soothes a child's soul. A grown-up is running the family, the way God intended it, and the children benefit, though they may not know it or be able to pinpoint why they feel better. Their mood will say, "It's better this way." And someday you'll hear that in words or in a letter from college in their sophomore year.

TWO

Psychological Correctness and Other Disciplinary Worries

Parents worry. It's in our nature. Never-before-pondered "what-ifs" arrive with the first child and never leave. They just change form with each phase and stage. In fact, realistic worries are integral to good discipline. They motivate us to do the right thing, to take the tough stands, even when it's easier to parent otherwise.

A new generation of worries, however, is plaguing parents these days. It has arrived with the flood of "new and improved" child-rearing notions. These worries are not realistic. They are groundless. They do nothing other than erode parent self-confidence and peace of mind, both of which are crucial to good discipline.

Too Many of a Good Thing

Dear Dr. Ray,

My mom and dad were so much more sure of their parenting than I am, and they didn't have all the books I do. I have to admit, all these experts sometimes just confuse me.

Spinning

They confuse me, too. What you're experiencing I see countrywide: a dramatic erosion of self-confidence among parents, even the most conscientious, loving ones. Talk to any grandparent, and routinely you could hear something like, "You know, I raised five kids, and I don't remember having a fraction of the frustration with all of mine that my daughter (or son) is having with just a six-year-old and a three-year-old."

I am convinced that what is happening in our society today is unprecedented in human history—that so many grown-ups are so tentative, or guilt-ridden, or lost, or all of the above, over raising children.

Picture the scenario. You're in a restaurant with your spouse, alone, for the first time in three years. Finally you found an adolescent willing to baby-sit for forty bucks an hour plus benefits. All you want is a little peace.

Glancing at the entrance, you see my wife and me walk in with our ten children, ages fifteen to three (it's true, we do this sometimes). Is your immediate response, "Is that precious or what? Oh, waitress, please ask that family to sit here next to us so I can enjoy their interplay for the next two hours"? Or do you think, "Oh help, how did they get past security?"

I would submit that most people think the latter. And not because they see ten kids; they could see only two and still think this way. Why? Because it is more than likely that experience tells them those two big people will be unable, or unwilling, to control those little people enough to keep them from disrupting their meal and everybody else's meal within fifty feet.

30

What has changed from only a generation or two ago to now? We could talk for hours about all the factors undercutting good parents today, but for the moment I'll focus on a major one: me. Put more broadly: the experts.

We're everywhere—swarming talk shows, magazines, pouring out thousands of books. We've taken over parenting, at least "enlightened" parenting. Our overall message may be unintended, but nonetheless, it's real: "Yes, parent, you can muddle your way along. Hopefully your child won't need too much therapy in her forties. But to be an up-to-date, psychologically correct mom or dad, you'd better follow the latest state-certified, congressionally mandated, on-the-air, child rearing advice."

Am I exaggerating? Maybe for emphasis. But I've struggled for years trying to comprehend why otherwise intelligent, competent grown-ups routinely get buffaloed by even the littlest kid. And I've concluded that the relentless waves of permissive and often contradictory child rearing notions have taken an enormous toll on what was once basic common sense and healthy parental authority.

So how can you reverse your slide into uncertainty? Always keep several realities at the forefront of your parenthood.

1. *You are the parent in your family; they are not.* Not Dr. Yule Feelgood, not Aunt Intrusa, not little Damien, but you. Heed advice as you wish—that's my advice—but realize that ultimately all decisions are yours, based upon what's best for you, your child, and your family.

2. *Keep your moral goal in mind: What are you trying to teach?* So much of parenting is not about what is psychologically correct, but what is morally correct. If, say, you value humility over self-esteem, or gentleness of spirit over assertiveness, this will render much expert advice quite irrelevant to your child's character formation.

> **So much of parenting is not about what is psychologically correct, but what is morally correct.**

3. *Focus on effectiveness.* What works is generally more valuable than what sounds psychologically slick, or theoretically new and improved. Much is to be said for the wisdom of generations. It's been gathered through long centuries of reality.

In the end, why should you listen to me? After all, I'm one of those experts. True, but I am trying to put authority and self-confidence into your hands, where it belongs. So someday your kids, too, will say, "My mom seemed so sure of herself ..."

Prescription Parenting

Dear Dr. Ray,

I recently read that parents should compliment their children three times as much as they correct. Doesn't that seem simplistic and rigid?

Mothering by Numbers

Formula child rearing. The new, up-to-date, improved way to raise kids. You've come across but one small example in the relentless tide of psychological correctness, a movement that is threatening to turn parenthood into a series of techniques and prescriptions for insuring the outcome of a well-adjusted, competent child.

And the formulas are multiplying: one ask, one warn, one tell; more "I" messages than "you" messages; one minute for every year of age in time-out (or is it one year for every minute of age? I get that one all confused). However well-intentioned, too many experts are laying out their own personal yardsticks by which parents can measure their degree of modern, psychologically savvy child skills.

Solid parenthood will always be grounded on the intangibles: love, good judgment, morals, and common sense.

Even the word "parent" suggests this trend. It can now be a verb, as in "to parent," or "to apply the proper ideas and approaches." What used to be considered primarily a relationship infused with love, supervision, discipline, and openness is increasingly being codified into what are "appropriate parenting practices" (such as active listening, time-out, "I" messages) and "inappropriate" ones (spanking, saying no to a toddler, written apologies).

Certainly parents need skills and experience and practice. They must be willing to learn, from everywhere, even experts. But solid parenthood will always be grounded on the intangibles: love, good judgment, morals, and common sense. These virtues resist being reduced to a simple set of do's and don'ts, applicable to all parents, all kids, and all situations.

In defense of the "three compliments for every correction" idea, the intent may have been to underscore a broader guideline:

Encourage and praise more than you discipline. Doubtless, this is tougher with some kids than others, but it's something to aim for. As we noted before, in general, the more you notice the good, the less you have to bridle the bad—up to a point, that is. But all kids will require some discipline, no matter how positive their parents may be.

Like you, I'm very uneasy with such numerical advice. It implies there is a correct "amount" of parenting practice, and that this amount applies pretty much across the board.

Even if this were true, what parent could keep track of the proper ratio for just one child, let alone two or more? I can picture my wife running to the refrigerator after every encouraging word to make a hatch mark in the appropriate column. Actually, after I told her about this idea, she did say, "That doesn't seem so tough," and then proceeded to tell my daughter, "Hannah, please eat your toast over the table … and I like your sweater, your teeth look clean, and I appreciate the way you're keeping your food in your mouth."

Maybe I could get her to use the three-to-one ratio with me. I'd even settle for two-to-one. Then again, maybe I haven't earned it.

Do Mistakes Make Maladjustment?

Dear Dr. Ray,

I guess I read too much. I'm always worried that I'm going to do something wrong as a parent, something that will cause emotional problems, now or later in life.

Tentative

Your question underscores what may be the most haunting fear among good parents today: the fear of making a child rearing "mistake" that will lay the groundwork for psychological damage. What's more tormenting is that you can't know when or where the damage will surface because it's buried deep within a youngster's psyche, festering for years until rearing its ugly head. And when it does, you have to wonder helplessly what you "did wrong."

Seventeen years from now, will your daughter be sitting in the middle of some "encounter group," along with seven other ex-embezzling parolees—she's their leader—talking about you and the turning point in her life? "I've never shared this with anyone before. I was barely five years old.

How can you possibly parent under the constant fear that if you miscalculate, misjudge, lose your cool, or make any other miscue, you run the risk of setting into motion an unseen chain of emotional events that will culminate in a social misfit?

"My mother was screaming my full name over and over from the garage, along with words I couldn't understand. When I answered, she said, 'Go to your room and don't come out until you're married.' Then she started throwing my Care Bear under the truck tires, driving back and forth over it, laughing hideously and promising that she'd never buy me anything ever again if I couldn't keep it where people wouldn't trip over it.

"I was never the same after that. When I was six, I wrote my first bad check. A year later, I started counterfeiting school lunch tokens."

How can you possibly parent under the constant fear

that if you miscalculate, misjudge, lose your cool, or make any other miscue, you run the risk of setting into motion an unseen chain of emotional events that will culminate in a social misfit?

Little Charity hates to share with her brother. If you make her do so, will she grow up hating all men?

The only way to get Newton to do his math homework is to require that he finish it immediately after school before he goes outside to play. He hates this rule and fights it. Will he eventually be so turned off toward numbers that he'll become a fifteen-year-old sixth-grade dropout?

Day-to-day parenthood requires so many decisions and judgments that you could keep yourself in perpetual turmoil second-guessing every move you make.

The experts have done a lot to scare parents. Recently, a "family specialist" on national television told parents that the absolute worst thing they could do to their children—it would lead to all manner of addictions and psychological imbalance—was to be inconsistent. Yet what parent isn't? In fact, what is one of the defining characteristics of human beings? Inconsistency.

Not one of us is even close to consistent in parenting or anything else. We may strive toward it, but we'll never get there. And now we've just been told that because we are what we are, we'll ruin our kids! One parent said to me, "Reading all this stuff makes me feel as if the worst thing for a child is a parent."

Parents must allow themselves to be human. Good parenting is a process of learning from good and bad moves alike. You'll make plenty of poor decisions. You'll say things you shouldn't. You'll overreact, denying John bathroom privileges for three months because he left his underwear on the towel rack again. (Of course, he'll use the standard paternal defense: "Dad leaves his underwear there, too." Not more than three seconds later, from the far corner of the garage, you'll both hear, "When you start paying the bills around here, young man, you can leave your underwear anywhere you want!")

Two other realities make it likely that, in sum, you will make more mistakes than your parents did, even if you're a better parent. The first is that childhoods are getting shorter. Nine-year-olds now face what twelve-year-olds a generation ago—what fifteen-year-olds two generations ago—used to face. The world is fast becoming a tricky, seductive place. If it's harder for children to grow up, it will be harder for parents to grow up with them, and more mistakes will be made along the way.

The second reality is this: While childhoods are getting shorter, parenthoods are getting longer. In past generations, after eighteen years or so the kids left to try life on their own. Nowadays, twenty-six or twenty-seven years after birth, they're still hanging around.

They might leave for a couple of years, just to tease you. But soon they're back, with their friends, and the bus, and their laundry, at 3:00 A.M., shouting, "No, guys, we can stay a little while, a couple of years anyway. Mom likes to cook big breakfasts and do laundry. She'll put food on the table between washing the white and color loads."

Parenthood is not for the faint of heart. It's as demanding as it is rewarding. In the end, the whole picture is what counts. And for most of us, the good moves far outnumber the bad.

It Ain't Over Till It's Over

Dear Dr. Ray,

I've read that a child's personality is pretty much formed by the age of five or six. That's a frightening thought.

Not Much Time

It sure is. Some years ago I was on a radio show talking about what makes a strong family. The instant we were on the air, the interviewer abandoned his prepared questions and blurted out, "Is it really true a child's personality is established by age five?"

Being a shrink type, and trained to answer questions with questions, I asked, "How old is your child?"

"Four," he said.

I reassured him, "Then you'd better drop those headsets right now and get home. You don't have much time left."

The notion that children are psychologically crystallized early in life is an old-timer among personality theories. Fortunately, time has shown it false. The research has concluded what common sense would: We unfathomably complex creatures cannot be explained by looking back to several, mostly lost to memory, early years.

I don't know about you, but I'm real different now from what I was when I was five. My wife says I have the maturity level of a nine-year-old. That's pretty high for husbands. When I teach my sons to burp the alphabet, I always make them say, "Excuse me," when they're done.

When you were five or six, did you have any political party

The grand psychological irony is that right when you're first learning your way around parenting, we experts comfort you with these thoughts: "These are the critical years. Bad moves now can reverberate well into Social Security."

affiliation? How about deep religious convictions? What qualities would you have valued in an older second-grade spouse? To be sure, many patterns begin and can be nurtured early, but to assert that Crystal is who she is now because of who she was in preschool not only defies reality, it needlessly frightens parents right when they're most vulnerable—in young parenthood.

Your first baby is a journey into uncertainty. How long do you let her cry? Is she hungry, wet, mad, hurting, spoiled? Who can always know? Often you guess. Feeding, sleeping, toilet training, disciplining—when, where, how much—all new turf.

The second-guessing can reach tormenting levels. If you leave him on the potty six minutes too long, will he grow up to be a tattoo-faced, purple-haired, spike-in-the-nose, afternoon-TV guest? And you were told to name him John to help in his toilet training!

It is not a stretch to say that early first-time parenthood is the peak period of insecurity for many parents. (Adolescence is a close second.) Yet the grand psychological irony is that right when you're first learning your way around parenting, right when you're most worried about mistakes, we experts come along and comfort you with these thoughts: "These are the critical years. Bad moves now can reverberate well into Social Security." One mother lamented to me, "Why couldn't the critical years be from ages ten to fifteen? I could get experience for a decade or so and then be ready."

Happily, for this mom and for all parents, personality is ever-evolving. Indeed, we have a lot more than five or six years to make mistakes. God willing, we can make them—and learn from them—through a whole childhood to raise great adults who can adapt to life and continue to change for the better.

I believe that, in general, the younger the children, the less they are affected by grown-up mess ups. First, younger kids are more emotionally resilient. They are more likely to overcome and leave behind whatever hurts and trauma may have entered their lives.

Second, on a more mundane level, half the time the little ones don't even realize what we're doing. Did you ever get a three-year-old mad at you? He stays upset for nearly six seconds until a fly buzzes past his face and he chases it, forgetting all about you and your awful discipline.

I once asked a group of parents, "When is personality truly complete?" A lady in the back raised her hand and offered, "When you're married?"

"No, ma'am," I replied. "When your life is over."

Without skipping a beat, she said, "Same thing." *Ouch.*

A Healthy Fear

Dear Dr. Ray,

I've heard experts say that children should never fear you or your discipline. Sometimes my son (age six) looks pretty scared when he's done something wrong and I've found out. Now I'm starting to feel guilty.

Fearsome

As we've noted, in some trendy child rearing theories, the word "discipline" has lately developed a bad reputation. The same has happened—just as undeservedly—with a few other once-respected words. Among the other terms most popularly disliked are "punishment" and "fear." The message is: If you are psychologically savvy enough, you'll seldom have to discipline, much less punish, and you'll never invoke fear.

On a recent television show I was debating the pros and cons of spanking with a childrearing specialist. (There's something odd about having so many specialists these days telling parents how do something correctly that they've been doing without us for millennia.) Violently anti-spanking, this expert asked me if I'd ever spanked my children. "Yes," I replied, "for certain misbehaviors."

She practically smacked me with her response: "Then your children must fear you."

Temporarily off balance, I replied, "How can you say something like that? You don't know me or my children. Besides, I want my kids to have a healthy fear of particular consequences. And since my wife and I are the ones to enforce those consequences, at times their fear might temporarily be attached to us. With maturity they'll come to understand the love behind our actions."

My reasoning didn't budge her. In her eyes, anyone who at any time for any reason swatted a bottom was a fear-monger. Period.

My wife and five-year-old son were watching the show at home. Turning to him, she asked, "Andrew, are you ever afraid of Daddy?"

"Nah."

I think his answer bothered me more than the expert's rebuke.

How often have you or another adult, after watching a child bullying his parents or being otherwise obnoxious, said something like, "If I'd have tried that with my parents, it would have been all over. I just knew better." Most parents with such recollections—often warmly recalled, by the way—grew up in loving homes.

Was fear a part of their discipline? Sometimes. It wasn't a fear that made them tremble when a parent walked by. It was a fear based on respect, not to mention wariness of the unknown: What would Mom or Dad really do if I was foolish enough to push them that far?

I have no fear of judges. I like them. Society needs them. Yet I'm very afraid of what they could do to me if I ever earned a visit to their courtroom as a criminal.

The fact that your son occasionally looks upset in the face of discipline is one sign he's developing a conscience. And as far as I'm aware, not too many are calling conscience bad—

not yet, anyway. A measure of fear and guilt, whether we like it or not, is inextricably tied to a healthy sense of right and wrong.

Because your son does worry about your reaction, say, if he leaves the yard without permission, he's less likely to wander away. Not only does he stay safe,

> **A measure of fear and guilt, whether we like it or not, is inextricably tied to a healthy sense of right and wrong.**

but you and he spend a lot less time wrangling over the issue. Your boundaries are clear; he knows that; and he's assured you'll back your words with action. Maybe his fear is better called a mature regard for reality.

The Spirit Isn't Weak

Dear Dr. Ray,

My four-year-old son, Jason, seems to get into far more than his share of trouble. To use a word, he is high-spirited. If I discipline him as much as he seems to need, will I break his spirit?

Cautious

Your Jason sounds like another little guy I met recently— David. David was the closest thing to perpetual motion I've seen in awhile. Indefatigable, he endlessly tampered with anything within eyesight to see how it could be taken apart or destroyed. He averaged 22.6 questions per hour, wanting the *why* of everything from the basic laws of physics to his parents' rules.

He was forever pitting his will against that of adults, sometimes to win, sometimes just to see what would happen.
Unfortunately, David's innate spunk coupled with his penchant for rule breaking led him to be the first child ever
"expelled" from his preschool. His mother's question mir-
rored yours: How do I teach self-control without breaking the
will?

To begin, kids who run on high idle, or who constantly challenge, or who buck every rule, almost always do need more
discipline than their more even-tempered or docile counterparts. Discipline itself does not break spirits. On the contrary,
it gives youngsters the self-control necessary to use their
inborn energy to its full potential.

Of course, your discipline has
to be more firm than the average parent's. You have to work
harder at sticking to your guns
and following through. Staying
calm is a daily challenge. In
short, a "high" (euphemism for
feisty) spirit tests a parent's spirit. But, believe it or not, it will
make you a better parent. And that leads directly to a better
child.

**A high spirit and self-control
are not mutually exclusive
characteristics. A child who is
born with the first and learns
the latter through his parents
will maximize both gifts.**

To maintain your parental sanity you need to decide when
to discipline and when to let Jason's exuberance feed itself
fully. Start with this guideline: If Jason's behavior is not hurting anyone, himself included, nor trampling on anyone's
rights, why intervene?

Whom or what is Jason harming by squirming through

forty-six contortionist postures per TV commercial, by asking Grandpa (who really doesn't mind) fourteen questions per minute, or by singing himself to sleep, however off-key? On the other hand, if the living room couch is Jason's practice trampoline, or Jason calls Grandpa "dumbhead" because he can only guess at twelve of fourteen questions, or sings right through your wishes that he at least be lying in bed by 8:00 P.M., then his actions are infringing upon others' rights, or are irresponsible, and need to be tempered or stopped.

Doing so does not break wills. It provides the guidelines that kids need to put direction to their spiritedness.

A high spirit and self-control are not mutually exclusive characteristics. Indeed, they complement each other well. A child who is born with the first and learns the latter through his parents will maximize both gifts.

THREE

Discipline: Acting, Not Yakking

Much of what looks like legitimate discipline is not. It is mere talk. Words, no matter how many, how logical, how emotional, how loud, can't replace real discipline: action. Eliminating counterfeit forms of discipline is a first step toward better discipline. And better discipline makes for a stronger and kinder parent. Less talk, more action—a time-tested discipline formula.

Talk: It's Cheap

Dear Dr. Ray,

I'm a mother of three children. It seems like I'm nothing but a talking machine. All the kids just shut me off. Any ideas for making myself heard?

Hoarse

Talk—the illusion of discipline. Nagging, lecturing, over-reasoning, pleading, cajoling, arguing, threatening, screaming are all forms of talk, all frustrating, and all imposters of legitimate discipline. I suspect the succinct adage, "Talk is cheap," was coined by a child.

As a kid, I liked it when my parents overtalked and said in

seventy thousand words what they could have said in seven. Playing in the backyard, I'd be blissfully ignoring my mother's repeated calls for supper when the torrent would come.

"Raymond Nicholas! How many times do I have to call you? You know, buddy boy, you seem to think I talk just to hear myself talk. You seem to think I like the sound of my own voice. Well, I'm going to tell you something, young man. You'd better listen and you'd better listen good because I'm not going to say it again. I was not put on this earth to serve you. There are five other people in this house. If you think we're going to revolve our schedule around yours, you've got another think coming. You mark my words, there's going to be some changes around here. I have just about had it with you. I'm sick and tired ..."

If you talk two hundred to four hundred words a minute, with gusts up to seven hundred, most of what you say is for your ears only, because a foremost reality of discipline is this: The more you talk, the less you're heard.

I never even looked toward the house until the 69,999th word. My attitude was, "She's not mad enough yet."

If you talk two hundred to four hundred words a minute, with gusts up to seven hundred, you can be sure of one thing: Most of what you say is for your ears only, because a foremost reality of discipline is this: The more you talk, the less you're heard.

A related reality is that the more space between your mouth and your kids' ears, the less you're heard, no matter how loud you get. It's just plain easier for D.J. to tune you out when you're standing across the backyard or even just across the hall than when you're looming right next to him. It's even easier to ignore you if you're out of sight, in other words, if there's a ceiling, wall, stairs, or a dirty window between you and him. Voices without faces have little meaning to kids who operate from the philosophy that "a parent should be heard and not seen."

The final futility of endless talking is that such talking inevitably leads to yelling, which inevitably leads to anger. We get riled, the kids get riled, the dog gets riled, and our original disciplinary purpose becomes lost in a maelstrom of words and emotion.

I've yet to meet a parent who can calmly say, "Please, Rose, this is the eleventh time I've asked you to water the flowers. Another ten or twelve times, and I'm afraid I'll have to raise my voice." For most of us, after four such requests, our voice volume is approaching 110 decibels and our jaw is so clenched we can't speak clearly anymore.

Why do we fall into the talk trap? First, talk is easier than action, in the very short term, anyway. Somehow we convince ourselves that it takes less effort to threaten Mercy sixteen times with an early bedtime if she blows her whistle a seventeenth time while we're on the phone than to leave the phone temporarily, pack her off to bed and weather twenty-seven minutes of crying. It probably does take less physical effort, but the emotional toll is much higher, not to mention still having to talk over that infernal whistle.

Second, talk usually makes us feel less guilty than actual discipline. We don't feel quite so "mean" nagging at Hazel through two game shows and a miniseries to clear the supper dishes as we would if we fined her fifty cents. Again, in the short run we may feel less mean. But soon we start feeling meaner and meaner as our words and polite requests go unheeded or challenged. And then our words can become meaner than a fifty-cent fine could ever be.

Third, kids are crafty. They want to keep us talking. They know that the longer we talk, the more likely we'll eventually wear down, give in, and shut up.

Of course, if all you have to do is smile sweetly while whispering, "Dishes please," and Chastity instantly drops the phone and rushes to dry them, then talk serves you well. Stay with it and savor the envy that all the rest of the world's parents feel toward you. On the other hand, if your words are having as much impact as Ping-Pong balls thrown at the hull of a battleship, then you need some action backing up your talk.

If-Then-Ing

Dear Dr. Ray,

You say that talk is cheap when it comes to discipline. Well, then, what should I be doing instead?

Ready to Rumble

Talk sounds like discipline, feels like discipline, and may at times work like discipline. But talk alone is a fraud. It's the grand illusion of discipline. And kids know it.

They realize this truth somewhere before their second birthday, or about the same time we parents are closing in on our one-hundred-thousandth discipline word. After only a few months, those who live near an airport become oblivious to the roaring jets passing overhead. Likewise, kids who live near roaring parents grow deaf to a stream of words passing overhead, even if some are whizzing by at six hundred miles per hour.

If you want to talk less and be heard more—nearly every parent's discipline dream—you can practice "if-thens." Instead of repeating sixteen variations of "Jay, quit putting oil in the birdbath," try saying one time, "Jay, if you put oil in the birdbath, you will clean it and spend the rest of the day inside." Other examples of *If-then-ing:*

- "Nielson, please turn off the TV and come to supper. If I turn it off, I decide when it comes back on."
- "Polly, this discussion is over. Don't say another word, or you'll cool down in your room."
- "Matt and Clay, please wipe your feet at the door. If you track dirt in, you'll vacuum the whole carpet."

If-thens can promise privileges as well as consequences:

- "Gardiner, if the lawn is mowed by 6:00 P.M., we may have time for some ice cream."

The *if-then* is a logical proposition. It tells the kids what you'd like and what will happen if they choose to ignore you. *If-then-ing* is a skill that gets better with practice. Here are ways to polish your skills:

1. Use "please" and "thank you." *If-thens* work best when said quietly and confidently. Courtesy will remind you to stay calm. What's more, the softer parents speak, the more kids listen. I think it has something to do with shattering their image of us.

2. Choose clear-cut consequences. "Dawn, you'd better get out of bed or else," invites Dawn to think, *Or else what?* You may get results the first few times, mostly through Dawn's fear of the unknown, but eventually she'll check out your "or else" for herself.

3. Don't threaten. "Art, you color on this table one more time, and you'll eat it and the tablecloth, too!" *If-thens* are not vengeful threats. They are matter-of-fact statements conveying a choice. They must be enforceable.

It is better to say nothing in the face of misbehavior and at least not lose credibility than to promise action you carry out only 13 percent of the time.

4. Follow through. The heart of the *if-then* is the *then*. It is the backup that makes your discipline true discipline and not just talk. Indeed, it is better to say nothing in the face of misbehavior and at least not lose credibility than to promise action you carry out only 13 percent of the time.

5. Don't reremind. Your kids know the consequences. They heard you the first time. Let your actions do your talking.

If-thens short-circuit the escalating spiral of harsh words and emotions that inevitably result when parents and kids become locked in verbal wrestling matches. They not only keep you from getting so riled you want to tear out your hair, and your kids', but they also keep the kids from reaching critical mass (a technical term meaning "about to explode").

If you can't think of *thens* as fast as your kids present you with *ifs* (the normal parent-child state of affairs) you have two options. One, don't say anything until you've thought of a *then.* Or two, make a list of all-purpose *thens* to fall back on when you're temporarily stumped—for example, half an hour in their room, sitting at the table with head down, or fifteen minutes' worth of chores. Good discipline isn't necessarily fancy. It is basic predictability.

If-thens are an extremely effective discipline technique. *If* they don't improve things within a year, *then* you might want to consider moving into the garage.

Word Storms

Dear Dr. Ray,

I'm a lecturer, and the kids are increasingly tuning me out. Is there hope to be heard?

Talk to Me

In my book *Back to the Family,* I interviewed strong families to find out what they were doing right. We also talked to the kids to hear what they liked—and didn't—about their family life. From the teens especially, the number-one ranked disliked parenting practice was lectures. Routinely, the kids admitted to drifting into a semiconscious state after about two minutes of a steady word stream. Two minutes is longer than it sounds when there's no break in the verbiage.

The propensity to lecture is a strong one and begins early

in parenthood. Once, when my oldest son was about four, my wife had sent him to his bed for lying. After I heard from her what happened, I figured I'd go up and add my fatherly two cents' worth, although I think the average lecture is about sixty-eight cents' worth.

"Andrew, Mom says you lied."

"I don't remember."

"Andrew, if Mom says you lied, you lied. Now I'm only going to ask you once for the truth. If you tell me the truth, you'll only stay here as long as Mom said. If you lie to me, too, you'll stay here even longer. Now, did you lie?"

The silence was broken only by the sound of mental wheels spinning. "I still don't remember, but if Mom says I did, there's probably a pretty good chance I did."

Aha, the parenting moment I'd been anticipating. My first chance to lecture, though I'm sure that's not what I would have called it. Mentally I'd been preparing for this rite of parental passage.

"Andrew, I want to talk with you a minute." Then I gave him my best stuff—I talked about trust, about God's rules about lying, about love. I even shared a touching story from my own childhood. Yes, our souls had met. Andrew would carry this memory of his dad for life.

About eight minutes into my monologue, and his silence, I stopped. "Well, Andrew, what do you think?"

"Dad?"

"Yes, Son."

"How come if I look up at the ceiling with one eye, my other eye can't look at the floor?"

Somewhere in my soul talk, I lost that boy, and I think it was probably when I said, "Andrew, I want to talk with you a minute."

Why do we persist in the face of overwhelming evidence that we're being tuned out, especially with teenagers, who are masters at turning to stone? Part of it has to do with our heart-deep drive to be good parents. We desperately want to make ourselves understood.

> If we can just get through to him, he'll see, and learn, and change, and be grateful to us, sometimes even saying, "Golly, Dad, thank you for talking at me for thirty-seven straight minutes. I needed that."

We know why we do or don't want Rock to do something. If we can just get through to him, he'll see, and learn, and change, and be grateful to us, sometimes even saying, "Golly, Dad, thank you for talking at me for thirty-seven straight minutes. I needed that."

Why are lectures generally so futile anyway? One, kids don't see parenthood through our eyes. The process of growing up takes years, and densely packed parenting words, however persuasive to us, don't do much to convince kids to think like adults. Some day most will, but not during a verbal storm, unless it's theirs.

Two, nobody—child or adult—likes to be on the receiving end of droning. Further, while most lectures may begin as drones, they don't stay that way. The longer they go, the more likely they are to become tirades.

Three, lectures are generally spawned by an emotional situation. Somebody—usually a juvenile—has behaved poorly, and somebody else—usually the juvenile's parent—is real upset, or hurt, or disappointed about it. The closer in time the lecture is to the trouble, the more likely emotions cloud clear thinking.

OK, so we all agree that, for the most part, lectures don't work. Once in a while, they may be heard and heeded, but the more words more often, the less impact. What can we do instead?

First, if you must lecture, keep it short. If it's short, it probably couldn't be called a lecture. Two to three minutes should be enough to get your point across.

Second, once you've expressed your thoughts and feelings, finish by explaining what you plan to do about this particular conduct. Focusing on consequences keeps a lecture from getting personal.

Finally, if your emotions are churning, delay the talk. Send Echo to her room while you cool. With lower emotional temperatures comes less push for steamy words.

Thank you for listening. I was hoping you would, though sometimes I'm pretty disappointed in how you react. After all I write for you, you'd think you'd care enough to read it. You know, not everybody is going to write for you all your life. You'd better get used to that fact, because I'm going to tell you something else ...

They Won't Listen Unless I Get Mad

Dear Dr. Ray,

My kids won't do anything I ask unless I yell. And they won't stop doing anything unless I yell some more. I'm getting louder by the day.

Old Yeller

One earmark of an addiction is habituation. In simple words, habituation means you need more and more of something to get the same effect. Even from this distance, it sure sounds like your kids have habituated to your normal tone of voice, thus pulling you into more and more volume to get a reaction.

I suspect you weren't always in such loud shape. At one time—though you might strain to remember—you were probably calm during most discipline. But if words acted as your discipline, and not consequences, then as usually happens, they lost impact.

So you were hooked into using even more and louder words to get yourself heard. Alas, habituation is a stubborn phenomenon. Once it grabs you, it's easy to use more of the same approach only to get more of the same response.

You see the end of all this. Yelling makes you feel mean and guilty, and your kids ignore you anyway. Nobody benefits. (Doesn't it seem that kids can outmaneuver us just by being themselves?) A nice thing about parenting, and discipline in particular, is that we get a lot of chances to get smarter.

So how do you withdraw from the yelling addiction? Probably the least painful way is to go cold turkey. Cease yelling and return to normal speaking volume.

I know, that's easier yelled than said. But to get Serena to hear soft words again you must start using soft words again. Otherwise, you'll just start yelling at her to listen when you talk softly.

Sometimes, merely talking softly works for awhile because it's such a shock to the kids' systems. They're so stunned they listen, if only in a mindless daze. Sometimes a quiet tone works because Everhard wonders why all of a sudden you're so calm. He's wary about what you're up to.

To paraphrase an old saying, one deed is worth one thousand decibels.

Then again, he might feel sorry for you. It's been years since you've talked so softly. Maybe you've finally cracked.

Even if the kids start to listen again, don't expect it to last. It's a honeymoon phase. To get durable listening, speaking quietly is only the first step. The second step is where you'll really make yourself heard.

You must provide a reason for your children to listen. In other words, you must make it in their best interests to heed you. How? By backing your quiet request with a quiet statement of the consequences for ignoring you. Examples:

- Hazel, please have your room cleaned by 6:00 P.M., or you'll stay there until it's spotless.
- Wyatt, don't squirt your water pistol at the dog, or you'll lose it for a week.
- Angela, please leave your brother alone, or you'll sit on the coach for twenty minutes.

To paraphrase an old saying, one deed is worth one thousand decibels. Your consequences are doing your talking, not your words. Will your kids ignore your quietly conveyed choices? Most likely. But in time they'll find out you mean what you softly say. You don't need volume to be reckoned with. You are willing to act in the event that diplomacy is unsuccessful.

Please try these ideas; they should help. I said, *try these ideas, they should help!* I'M TELLING YOU ONE LAST TIME, GIVE THESE IDEAS A TRY! I'm sorry. Let me try again. Please try these ideas, or I'm not going to answer your questions anymore.

Kid Logic

Dear Dr. Ray,

Any comebacks to kids who always seem to have a comeback to everything you say? I don't always know how to respond to their logic.

A Poor Debater

Socrates was a pretty bright guy, but he was never really challenged. He only argued with grown-ups who totally disagreed with him. He never had to match wits with a twelve-year-old who refused to understand why he wasn't allowed to stay out after dark.

The trouble with kid-logic is that it can sound rational, until you ponder it for three or four seconds. Certainly it makes perfect sense to the children using it. In their eyes, if our brain cells weren't so fossilized by age, we'd fully accept their flawless line of reasoning:

Sherlock: Why can't I stay out a half hour past dark?

Parent: Because it's not safe. For one thing, there are no people around.

Sherlock: If there are no people around, it's safer.

Parent: Why would you want to stay out after dark? None of your friends are allowed to.

Sherlock: That's why I want to. I think I need private times alone.

Parent: I just feel better when I know you're home safe.

Sherlock: Then why do you make me go to school?

Parent: That's completely different.

Sherlock: Yeah, it is. At school, I'm gone for six hours. After dark, I'm only gone for half an hour.

The only reasonable observation about this sort of discourse is that the longer it goes on, the more illogical it becomes. Put another way, the more we argue, the farther apart we get. There is no resolution because grown-ups and kids don't regularly think on the same plane. But kids are much better at pulling us down to their level than we are at pulling them up to ours.

Kids are much better at pulling us down to their level than we are at pulling them up to ours.

The most logical comeback to kid-logic is no comeback. End the exchange as quickly as possible. Even so, to paraphrase the poet, don't expect Sherlock to go quietly into that good night. He may rage against the dying of the fight. Getting to do what he wants is riding on his ability to fight unfair. Therefore, you may need a few debate-closing options.

Upon hearing resistance to your initial explanation, you might say, "I gave you my reason. You didn't like it." Then say no more. Asking yourself, "When was the last time I won one of these?" should help curb your urge to engage in any further word wrestling.

If you've reiterated the same theme for the same discipline 234 times in the past six months and you're beginning to feel just the slightest pangs of frustration, you'd probably best quietly walk away the instant the debate begins. This isn't rude; it's wise. Kid-logic breeds parent illogic, usually culminating in some outburst like "Because I said so, that's why!" or "When you have your house, you can run it your way" or "I can't wait until you have four kids just like you."

Careful on this last one. You'll be a grandparent to those kids. Do you want to be the one to baby-sit them?

One other technique is the ultimate in psychological sophistication: the stupid look. The moment kid-logic begins, stare dumbly. Granted, this is easier for some of us than others, but the stupid look is well worth any time it takes to master.

It wordlessly conveys, "Not only am I not going to argue, but I don't even understand what we would argue about." Teens especially quiet down in the face of a stupid look. I think it has something to do with their image of us.

One mother asked me, "What if you just naturally look stupid? How can your kids tell if you're reacting to them or just being yourself?" I had no idea how to answer that, so I gave her a stupid look.

Asking for Trouble

Dear Dr. Ray,

As a grandmother, I think too many parents these days are asking their children to cooperate rather than simply telling them what they expect. It sounds like they're constantly negotiating with their children.

Asking Your Opinion

Some years back, three of my children attended the same preschool class. Arriving a few minutes early to pick them up was wise, for a couple of reasons. One, I could observe the other parents for possible material to write about. Two, I could better ensure that my kids didn't have too much time to misbehave in front of everybody. After all, if my kids act bad in public, I could lose business.

What I heard confirms your sentiment. Routinely parents would query their kids: "Are you ready to go now?" "Come on, let's put our coat on, OK?" "Why don't you say goodbye to your teacher, all right?"

Putting expectations into question form is appealing. It sort of conveys a "let's all get along" approach. Overall it just makes us parents seem like nicer people, don't you think?

Now such questioning, even if it's a habit, provides nowhere near enough evidence to consider a diagnosis of *parentus maximus wimpus*. In fact, I would guess that most of these parents were just wanting to convey a pleasant, "Let's cooperate ... OK?" tone. To the extent that they got cooperation, I would never question their style, do you understand?

What I saw from the kids, however, was not cooperation. It wasn't an attitude of "Why thank you, Mother, for asking so sweetly. It just makes me want to listen all the more." Instead, I saw a reaction of "You're not really all that serious, are you?"

Putting expectations into question form is appealing. It does sound rather gentle and less "bossy." It sort of conveys a "let's all get along" approach. Overall it just makes us parents seem like nicer people, don't you think?

But traps lie beneath the surface benefits. One, questions invite resistance. If Sherlock takes our question literally, he could respond, "No, I'm not ready to go now. It's not our coat. It's my coat. You can put yours on if you want. And I don't feel like saying goodbye to my teacher, got it?"

Two, this sort of "question discipline" sends a message most parents don't mean to send. It makes expectations that are really nonnegotiable sound open to discussion. I mean, does Taylor really have a choice about putting on his coat and leaving?

Three, and this is potentially the biggest danger, if a child senses, even incorrectly, that a parent may not mean what he or she says, the child will likely ignore or resist the request, thus pushing the parent into command mode. In and of themselves, commands are not bad. The trouble comes from the struggle now to get cooperation, after implying initially it wasn't all that important. This then leads to frustration, emotions, and volume.

In essence, question discipline can easily evolve into bossy, mean discipline, the very thing the parent unconsciously may have been trying to avoid in the first place.

Certainly every mom and dad has the right to discipline as they see fit. And question discipline can work for some kids— mostly the sweet-natured Chastity and Oxford types.

Overall, though, my experience is that it's better quietly, confidently to state your expectations from the very start. It leaves little room for doubt. It reinforces your role as authority. In the long run, it really is a nicer way to discipline.

So why don't we all just try to do a little better on this, OK?

Whys Aren't Always Wise

Dear Dr. Ray,

Every time I ask my six-year-old, Joshua, why he did something, he answers, "I don't know." Is it possible he really doesn't know why he does what he does?

In the Dark

I don't know. But I do know that "Why did you do that?" or something similar is the most common brand of question parents ask kids. Ironically, it's also the brand of question that gets the fewest answers.

Your Joshua must be a pretty bright little guy, because he at least gives you an "I don't know." With most six-year-olds, a typical exchange goes something like this:

Mom: Sherlock, why on earth would you carve your initials into the aluminum siding one day after we put it up?

Sherlock: (Partial blank stare, as if to say, "What aluminum siding? What initials?")

Mom (trying again): If you don't know, who knows?

Sherlock: (Full blank stare, now directed toward his shoelaces.)

Mom (resorting to multiple choice, she provides the answers; all Sherlock has to do is pick one): Were you mad because I made you stay inside yesterday? (Silence.) Do you want to be like Delbert, who does anything he pleases? (Deadly silence.) Did you want to show me how well you can write cursive? (Deafening silence.)

Mom (one last desperate attempt): Sherlock, I'm so mad I can't see straight. But if you give me one good reason for those initials, I'm not even going to punish you.

That's the one I'd hold out for. And then I'd probably make something up: "Mom, you remember that time when I was four that I burped spaghetti sauce on Sheila's head and you dragged me by the ear all the way to my bedroom? Well, that's why. I've been holding that in for two years."

If a first or second *why* gets no answers, *whys* #3 through #36 are likely to meet the same fate. So why (there's that word again) do we persist in asking? For a couple of reasons.

We mistakenly assume that psychologically savvy parents always understand their children. Actually, psychologically savvy parents understand that some ignorance is a part of normal parenthood.

First, a widely held parenting notion is that we must know why kids do what they do in order to change it. Fortunately, that's not true. You just can't always figure out kids. And for most day-to-day mischief, their motives aren't fancy. They're usually some combination of the big three: I felt like it; my friends do it; I thought for sure I could get away with it.

The second reason for wanting the *why* is purely personal: It drives us crazy not to fathom the motive behind puzzling, unpredictable, or just plain nutty behavior. We mistakenly assume that psychologically savvy parents always understand their children. Actually, psychologically savvy parents understand that some ignorance is a part of normal parenthood.

Why do kids keep their reasons to themselves? Sometimes they really don't know why they did what they did. Insight into one's motives is a skill that comes with maturity. We adults don't always possess it. Sometimes kids are embarrassed by their reason ("I hit her because she sneezed").

Most often, silence is their best defense. You're already so incensed over Joshua's shaving the dog's tail, he figures he'll only compound his troubles by giving you his childish reason. If you're feeling merciful, at best he'll be shot at sunrise. So the standard kid motto is "When discipline is looming, don't admit to anything."

Certainly you can ask why once or twice, but if no response is forthcoming (the typical initial *why* failure rate is 77.23 percent), my advice is to drop the interrogation. Let Joshua know that it would be in his best interests to supply some method to his madness—it may provide mitigating circumstances—but you're not planning to haul out the bright lights to wrench it out of him.

With a six-year-old, a more fruitful question to ask is this: What did you do? Besides being an easier question for him to answer, it's an easier question for you to answer. You know what he did. You can see the spray paint on the garage walls. Can you be so sure of yourself with why questions?

To be sure, some kids won't even answer "What did you do?" Instead, they plead, "I didn't do anything." He's lived in your house for six years and not once has he ever done anything.

A second question to ask is "What happens when you do that?" or "What should we do about that?" Of course, Josh is thinking to himself, *What do you mean "we"? It won't be you who loses TV for a week. You won't be helping me scrub the garage walls.*

The point you're making is that there will be consequences

for such behavior, even if neither of you understands it. Placing consequences on irresponsible, destructive, or nasty behavior is generally more important, and easier, than getting a youngster to identify motives.

There's a bright side to not knowing why. Sometimes we're better off in the dark, because our kids' motives might scare us, confuse us further, or really make us mad. As my mom used to warn me, "Don't tell me why. I'm upset enough already!"

FOUR

Discipline: The Basics

I have good news and I have bad news. The good news is that discipline is founded upon a few easy principles. The bad news is that to make discipline easy, you have to work hard at it. Still, effective discipline is not psychologically fancy. It is the willingness to persevere with some pretty straightforward approaches. Getting good at something starts with mastering the basics.

On Being Consistent

Dear Dr. Ray,
  How can I be more consistent in my discipline?

  Consistently Inconsistent

Consistency. Talk about good discipline, and this word will appear in the first sentence or two. It's a discipline catchword, yet its meaning is slippery. Is consistency say-what-you-mean-and-mean-what-you-say? Is it follow-through? Is it predictability?

Actually, it's some measure of all these. For our purposes, let's say consistency means *reacting similarly to a recurrent behavior.* In other words, if Constance does x, we do y. Most of the time, anyway.

One-hundred-percent consistency is not possible, not as

long as parents are disciplining kids, and it's not something easy—such as untamed circus tigers. Nor is total consistency desirable. Sometimes flexibility is the wiser course.

Harmony came home forty-five minutes past curfew, thirty of which was due to a stalled train. She would have been late anyway, and you could further argue that she never leaves even thirty seconds leeway for an unplanned red light. Still, this may be an occasion to consider softer consequences, if nothing else but to show you can be merciful.

Somewhere around 60 percent consistency would seem an attainable goal. Most of us hover between 20 and 40 percent, with acceptable results. If this sounds low, consider: If you tell Neilsen three times to turn off the TV, and do nothing but talk, your consistency has already fallen to 33 percent. Children are masters at training parents to drop their rate of consistency this low and even lower.

How consistent you need to be is inextricably tied to the personality of your child. Butkus can be nudged along with an average 19 percent follow-through on your part. Harmony makes you reach 60 percent before even acknowledging you're in the same room.

Consistency is indispensable to competent parenting. First, it takes some of the guesswork out of misbehaving. The more certain Polly is of our reaction (for example, a blank stare) to her action (begging for gum in the checkout line), the sooner she'll cease pestering.

Second, consistency takes some of the guesswork out of discipline. We don't endlessly struggle to figure out "what now?" every time Eve nags for a second pitcher of water at bedtime. We know what now. Three weeks ago we decided to close the bedroom door at the first sound of badgering after bedtime.

There's a surprising relationship between disciplinary consistency and disciplinary frequency. As consistency goes up, frequency goes down. If, for example, you discipline only 20 percent of the time that discipline is called for, in the long run you will end up disciplining far more often, because a child will be quicker to test your limits. On the other hand, if you are 70 percent consistent (very high indeed), you will discipline much less. Kids are reluctant to ask for something they don't want but are really likely to get.

Striving for consistency is probably the hardest thing parents try to do on a daily basis. There is only one thing harder: being inconsistent.

Kids may be childish, but they're not dumb, especially in their knowledge of us. If Knight is sure that strolling in after dark will lead to a three-day grounding, and that we will *not* relent after one day, no matter how much he tries to punish us for our perseverance, he will be less likely to test our resolve the next time the sun sets.

One last point. Striving for consistency is extremely hard work. In fact, it's probably the hardest thing parents try to do on a daily basis.

There is only one thing harder: being inconsistent.

Playing the Odds

Dear Dr. Ray,

Trying to be consistent in my discipline exhausts me. It seems I'm on my kids constantly.

Constantly Tired

Though we know that consistency makes discipline less necessary, the problem is that most of us parents dramatically overestimate how consistent we are. This is not so much a criticism of our parenting as it is a comment on the weakness of human nature. We are innately inconsistent creatures. Because good child rearing demands consistency, it aims a floodlight on our human weakness.

To get an estimate of your consistency level, try this exercise. (Brace yourself, the numbers may not be pretty.) Consider your most challenging child, the one who pushes hardest, resists most, and frustrates your best parenting efforts. Think of the neighbor kid if you have to. The experts would variously tag this child oppositional, strong-willed, or difficult. In reality, most likely he or she's just a kid who's feistier by nature than his or her siblings.

On average, how many times a day does this child get disciplined—that is, experiences an actual consequence. He or she heads for the corner, is fined twenty-five cents for neglecting a chore, writes an apology, goes to bed early, loses a privilege. Most parents would answer: anywhere between zero and two times. Those with true Spikes and Spikettes may reach three or four.

The second question: On average, how many times a day does this child ignore you, defy you, throw a fit, torment a sibling, break a house rule, badger you, slough responsibilities? In other words, how many times a day does he or she misbehave, as you define it?

Most parents respond with some version of this: "Yeah, right. Do you want it to the nearest hundred? The numbers aren't too high at night, when she's asleep; Wait, let me get my calculator; it goes up to six figures." After we get down to hard numbers, most totals fall between twenty and fifty. Indeed, twenty is not all that much. If a child is home all day, twenty breaks down to about two incidents per waking hour.

Now, take the daily average of times when discipline is actually administered—let's use the high number, say two. Then divide that by the lowest misbehavior number, say twenty. Answer: 10 percent. That is the discipline consistency level, the percentage of times that an actual consequence follows misbehavior. Scary, isn't it?

Of course, I don't know what your personal consistency numbers are. But if you're feeling as if you're on the kids constantly, your words may fast be replacing action, and your consistency ratio will plummet. Once again, though, let me share some good and bad news.

The bad news is that kids are gamblers. If they sense that the odds of being held accountable for their behavior are acceptably low, they'll play the parental slot machine with more frequency and fervor. They'll take an occasional loss as the cost of doing kid business, which is to do as they wish, not as you wish.

If you're feeling as if you're on the kids constantly, your words may fast be replacing action, and your consistency ratio will plummet.

The good news is that with practice your discipline ratio can improve. And believe it or not, most children respond pretty well to a 30 or 40 percent consistency level. In fact, 30 percent would put you among the disciplinary elite.

Keep on Persevering

Dear Dr. Ray,

Though most experts emphasize the importance of consistency in good discipline, I've heard you talk about perseverance as well. Is it just as important?

Hanging in There

The value of perseverance depends solely on one question: Perseverance in what? Perseverance in nagging, reminding, cajoling, pleading, overreasoning, threatening, and emotional assaults is worse than worthless. It is counterproductive. It simply prolongs bad discipline habits that will teach Constance to persevere in ignoring or defying us. Excess words are the illusion of real discipline, so perseverance in talk leads mostly to frustration, for both parents and kids.

In short, when it comes to discipline, perseverance in mere words is bad.

Perseverance is good—indeed, it's of the highest value—when its partner is consistency as we have defined it: reliably placing consequences upon misconduct. In that case, then perseverance is consistency over time, sometimes a very long time. Perseverance is the willingness to do what it takes for as long as it takes to teach the desired lesson.

Let's say that talking on the phone is a challenge for you, not because you're socially awkward, but because your kids are like Pavlov's dogs. The bell rings, and they get rude, rowdy, and interrupt so much so that you salivate in anger. Enough of this, you've decided.

"Alexander, Belle, we have a new house rule. When I am on

the phone, you will be respectful. If not I will calmly excuse myself from the call, then escort you to your rooms for the rest of the call and maybe then some. Please don't resist, get louder, or come out. You'll be grounded for the day if you do."

How long will you have to persevere in enforcing your rule before you get peace on the phone? Twenty-five calls? Fifty-five calls? Two hundred and fifty-five calls? I really can't predict. And at one level the number is not relevant. Your goal is to do what you said. In time (2023?) your kids win learn to cooperate.

> A simple approach used consistently and with stick-to-it-iveness almost always works better than the most brilliant approach tried erratically or briefly.

Routinely I tell my clients, "One of the easiest parts of parent counseling is giving you ideas. I can give you many discipline ideas for any one problem. What I can't give you is the will to persevere. That is the crucial ingredient in seeing positive change." A simple approach used consistently and with stick-to-it-iveness almost always works better than the most brilliant approach tried erratically or briefly.

Let's get back on the phone for a minute. Good, durable discipline will keep the following from happening.

Rrriiinnnggg.

"Oh, hello, Deacon ... Well of course, we would be flattered to be the role model family for the church-children love-in ... (Glaring at the brawling children.) Deacon, could you please excuse me for one minute? I'm going to have a little love chat with the children. Oh yes, they're precious blessings from God ... Why certainly, after I encourage them, I'll get them on the phone to hear the good news, too ..."

With mouthpiece covered, teeth gritted, a guttural growl is

aimed at Alexander and Belle: "Get away from each other, you little brats. When I get off this phone, you'll both be sorry you got out of bed this morning. I mean it, you are both toast."

Drawn back to the phone now. "What's that, Deacon? No, that's the neighbor lady. She always talks to her children that way. Yes, we will pray for her; she needs prayers ... We have moved, but she keeps finding us!"

Perseverance in real discipline—calm, resolute action— leads to less discipline. Perseverance in fake discipline—lots of words powered by emotions—leads to more discipline. Perseverance is only valuable in pursuit of real discipline.

Changing Our Minds: A Parent's Prerogative

Dear Dr. Ray,

Is it appropriate to change your mind about your discipline, or would that be inconsistent?

Reconsidering

I used to think so, but I've since changed my mind. By "change your mind," I assume you mean, after the heat of a discipline moment has passed, to have second thoughts about your decision, or style, or both. That's what most parents mean.

Let's say Barney has just tormented his brother, Andy, for the umpteenth time today. In a fit of frustration, you levy a heavy fine: "I don't want either of you breathing within a mile of each other for two days, and if you do, you'll be grounded for a week."

Two hours later, Barney's in bed, asleep, looking cherubic, and you're calm, wondering how to get out of the corner you painted yourself into without looking wishy-washy or inconsistent.

First of all, it is neither weak nor inconsistent to reconsider logically a decision made during a burst of emotion. If later you conclude a lesser punishment would better fit the crime, this is not backtracking. Let's call it reassessing based upon—and this is key—a clearer perspective. Discipline will still happen, only in a more measured way.

It is never wrong to admit your own misbehavior. It's mature. Admitting your own childishness can help your kids grow up.

Second, if you've laid down a pretty foolish law, such as "no contact within a one-mile radius," you'll look even more foolish trying to enforce the unenforceable. Unless your house is absolutely enormous, or really tall, your discipline is pure fiction. Better to cut your losses, salvage your credibility, and tell them you meant "within a yard" of each other.

There's still a consequence, only now it's realistic. Kids love to push us to wild overstatement, and then watch us wriggle around on our own words.

Then, too, sometimes logistics dictate a discipline turn. A one-week grounding may burden you more than them. Figure out something else to substitute. Your discipline is still in force; the consequences have been changed to protect the innocent—you.

Third, be ready to apologize for verbal or emotional overkill. Your discipline itself may have been right on target, but your style was rough. You got personal or off the real point. It is never wrong to admit your own misbehavior. It's mature, even merciful. Admitting your own childishness can help your kids grow up.

Finally, real inconsistency in discipline comes from a pattern of poor follow-through due to laziness, guilt, fear of disapproval, weakness of will, or fatigue from being badgered. In other words, inconsistency arises from all the wrong reasons. It is not inconsistent to correct or tinker with a decision, provided you're not doing so out of a misguided sense of self-doubt.

For that reason, be open to a change of mind when you, through calm deliberation, determine it's called for. You will neither lose credibility nor send your kids the wrong message. Indeed, I think you'll rise in their eyes. They'll know that you're willing to think things over because *you* think it's warranted, not because *they* do.

Misbehavior and Misbeliefs

Dear Dr. Ray,

Staying calm is one of the hardest things for me to do when I discipline. How can I keep my cool?

Little Cool Left

Calm and discipline—two words that aren't often found in the same sentence for most of us parents. Not that we don't try to discipline calmly. It's just incredibly difficult, especially when the object of our discipline is a child, and not something

Not that we don't try to discipline calmly. It's just incredibly difficult, especially when the object of our discipline is a child, and not something easy, like a timber wolf.

easy, like a timber wolf. Complete calm during all discipline moments is unattainable, but it is a goal to work toward, for several reasons.

One, the more upset we get, the more likely our kids will act the same. (Did you ever notice how much more quickly kids imitate our bad habits than our good ones?) With everybody mad at everybody, things get said that aren't meant, and any real discipline rapidly gets lost in the emotional storm.

Two, our anger conveys a false message to our youngsters: "*I* am responsible for your behavior, not *you.*" It was young Forbes who stomped away from the family's monthly Monopoly game after landing on his sister-owned Boardwalk, but we're the ones who get most upset about his conduct.

Three, kids draw energy from their parents' anger. It gives them power over us. They act bad and we get mad.

When I was about six or seven years old, my mother's emotions would nearly reach hurricane force before she finally put me in my room. My attitude was "OK, Mom, I'll do my fifteen minutes; I ruined your day." Sometimes it's worth being punished just for the chance to get the folks so agitated.

When kids act up, parents often make themselves feel worse by misinterpreting the behavior. Here are three of the most common misbeliefs about misbehavior.

1. *My youngster's behavior is a reflection of my parenting.* Not necessarily so. Kids, being human beings—well, most of the time—act through their own wills.

You might be Parent of the Decade in the Western Hemisphere, but Igor can still work to make you lose the title. Why? Because he's a kid, and by his nature he is impulsive, childish, and shortsighted.

As a parent, you can respond to misconduct, but you can't totally prevent it. The ultimate responsibility lies with Igor. You provide the choices and consequences. He makes the decisions.

2. *This behavior is directed at me personally.* I don't say this to make you feel neglected, but most kids aren't even thinking about their parents when they're acting up. They may be forced to think about us after the fact, as they're straining to concoct some reason for wandering in at 1:15 A.M. or for not being at the library as promised, but immediately prior to their impulsive moves, they're not giving our feelings much thought.

If they were considering how we'd react, they'd be less likely to test us, wouldn't they? Kids are kids (we psychologist types are trained to say profound things) and their kiddish conduct is most often aimed at getting them what they want—not at us. If they upset us in the process, that's just a bonus.

3. *This behavior is a sign of things to come.* Rob has just stolen a match box Corvette from the store. Does this mean he will steal a real Corvette fourteen years from now? Absolutely not.

It is psychologically impossible to predict the future of a child based on one, two, or even several incidents of misconduct. This misbelief can torment parents more than any other. How can we calmly deal with a here-and-now incident of petty thievery when inside our own psyche all manner of "What if?" and "What does this mean?" questions are swirling around.

Always remind yourself that no one except God can know what any given behavior will lead to years from now. What's more, most misbehavior means *nothing* for the future. It is *right now* misconduct that must be handled *right now*. Peering ahead to guess about the long-term ramifications of some disturbing incident will only make you feel needlessly frightened and guilty.

There is a bright side to losing your cool. Anger is like a spice. If not overused, it can add memorable flavor to your discipline. Your kids will realize that when you do get angry, you're in no mood to mess around.

Lengthening Your Fuse

Dear Dr. Ray,

I've heard that we shouldn't discipline our children when we're angry. How can I do that? I find myself becoming more easily frustrated with my sons, ages nine and thirteen.

Trip Switch

Parents face a lot of subtle pressure these days to practice 100 percent anger-free child rearing. Resist the pressure. It can't be done.

No parent disciplines without getting angry sometimes. I do recall one mom who was determined to stay calm from day one of motherhood. She was eventually hospitalized with an ulcer, but her sixteen-month-old was allowed to visit her.

Anytime your emotions are wrapped tightly around another

human being, you will do emotional things, such as saying words you don't really mean, losing control, and yelling. Emotions, even negative ones, are signs of close involvement.

This said, most of us admit we could do a calmer job of child raising, disciplining in particular. Your question has many answers. For now, let's focus on one attitude crucial to calmer discipline.

Consider that even if a youngster were to misbehave only once per day (let me study such a child!) in sixteen years the total misbehaviors would be more than five thousand.

Consider the parenting debut. On day one, we are blessed with a being with zero social skills. It is completely self-centered. It wants what it wants the second it wants it, becoming a raving emotional lunatic if it doesn't get it. Over the better part of the following two decades we strive to permeate this child with self-control, maturity, and morals. In the meantime we face thousands upon thousands of episodes of resistant, obnoxious, difficult, thoughtless, moody, selfish behavior.

This isn't an overly negative picture. It's reality. It's childhood. And lest you think that "thousands upon thousands" is an overstatement, consider that even if a youngster were to misbehave only once per day (let me study such a child!) in sixteen years the total misbehaviors would be more than five thousand.

The more we understand and accept this fact of child rearing, the better we'll be able to confront it when it presents itself daily, even hourly or minutely.

A great definition of stress says that stress is the difference between the way we'd like things to be and **To keep frustration** the way that they are. To the degree that we **lower, act quicker.** expect a Hallmark card family scene with an ever-cooperative and grateful little Chastity and Oxford walking with us, we will be frustrated and wonder, "What's wrong?" The truth is that when kids misbehave, most of the time there's *nothing* wrong. They're being kids, and they're forcing us to be parents.

Once we have realistic expectations, we need a few techniques to lengthen our fuse. Here they are:

Technique #1. Act early in the chain. An all-too-typical disciplinary scene unfolds this way:

Butkus ignores, defies, or debates parent. Parent repeats him- or herself, prods, argues, threatens. Butkus resists further, talks tougher, escalates. Parent stands ground, gets upset, disciplines.

The whole scenario takes twenty-seven minutes to intensify. By the time the parent finally disciplines, the misbehavior has multiplied, words have clashed, emotions have fumed. Who wouldn't be frustrated at this point?

Don't allow the exchange to get on a roll. Discipline early, when it is warranted and while you're still calm. Believe it or not, Butkus will more quietly accept his discipline. To keep frustration lower, act quicker.

Technique #2. Get out of each other's faces. As soon as you feel your temperature rise a few degrees, send Butkus to his room before you act rashly, or you go to yours. The situation will still be dealt with, only later when you're back to 98.6°. Distance is a great sedative. It helps clear minds, stabilize reasoning, and soften words.

Technique #3. Delay. If a particular problem or misbehavior is unexpected, baffling, or worrisome, it doesn't need to be faced instantly. It's done now, and there's no real hurry to correct it. So put a little time between your discovery of the misconduct and your response to it. Like distance, time tranquilizes emotions. Not all the way, but enough to balance your feelings with thought.

Technique #4. Drop your voice. John Wayne's acting advice is sound advice for parents: Talk low, talk slow. Force yourself to speak more deliberately even as you feel less deliberate.

No parent can ever be calm all the time. Nor do I think you would want to be. Emotion makes a strong statement. The problem comes when emotion rules too often.

FIVE

Discipline: Multipurpose Consequences

The average child can misbehave faster than the average parent can think of how to discipline. So, if they are faster, we need to be smarter. Part of being a better disciplinarian is knowing how we will react to trouble before it starts.

That's why it's real savvy to have at the ready standard rules and consequences for a youngster's favorite misbehaviors. Kids can act up in thousands of ways. Fortunately, we don't need to have thousands of different responses. Some solid, workhorse consequences can successfully cover much day-to-day misbehavior.

K.I.S.S.

Dear Dr. Ray,

You often suggest using sitting in the corner as discipline for preschoolers and writing an essay on their conduct as discipline for older children. What are your reasons?

Mom of Both Ages

Why use these techniques? Simple: They're simple. Complex discipline approaches or fancy psychological tacks run headlong into an inescapable reality—human nature. There is a longstanding law of discipline, which I just made up: The simpler the discipline, the more likely we are to do it. The more likely we are to do it, the better it works. The better it works, the less we have to do it.

Today's over-psychologized parenting landscape is buried in the idea that elaborate is better.

"Get a four-foot-by-eight-foot sheet of butcher paper. Divide it into 1,044 squares. Each square represents fifteen seconds. If the child behaves well for fifteen seconds, put a checkmark in the square. When he behaves for ten squares in a row, reward him with a banana sticker. Ten stickers lead to a banana bunch that's placed on the refrigerator. For each bunch, the child may choose out of five hundred rewards you've compiled in a picture scrapbook, after interviewing the child, his friends, grandparents, teacher, probation officer, and all significant others for ideas. Now, to make the system really work, next you need to ..."

> The simpler the discipline, the more likely we are to do it. The more likely we are to do it, the better it works. The better it works, the less we have to do it.

Who can maintain a strategy like that for any amount of time?! The only people with this kind of energy and stamina have no children. This is why refrigerators are monuments to dead sticker systems. How many parents have begun some daily sticker reward system designed to, say, get Hazel to do her chores, only to have it work miraculously the first nine days and then fade into discipline oblivion?

Likewise, as children get older, the more complex our discipline, the more likely we are to exhaust, forget, relent, or get confused.

"OK, now does Nielson get TV back tomorrow at 6:00 A.M.

or 6:00 P.M., and is that Eastern or Mountain Time? Is it before he's allowed to ride his bike again, or did his going to bed early last night count as one day bike reprieve because he helped with the dishes right after he came down from time-out in his room because he was mad for being grounded after he got disrespectful because I told him to help his sister with her chores because he was nasty to her friend for teasing him about having to clean his room because ..."

Now, I'm not saying that fancy can't work, or that lots of different consequences necessarily breed inconsistency. But overall, the dictum *K.I.S.S.*—keep it short and simple—is wise advice for disciplining kids. It's easier on our heads (more certainty), our hearts (less guilt), our wills (greater perseverance), and our homes (blessed peace).

For instance, consider the basic go-sit-in-the-corner discipline. Corners are ubiquitous. They're everywhere. The average room has four of them. And for those of us with large families, if we fill up one room, we've got others. (This is a chronic problem in our home, as our corners can get backlogged. So I've taken a page from the justice system's manual: I hand the kids a sheet of paper that says, "Report next Wednesday at 2:00 A.M.; you have corner time." Also, to alleviate corner overcrowding, we've been forced to develop a halfway couch program.)

Essays, too, possess corner-like benefits. They can be assigned anytime, anywhere, any length. You can choose the topic—talk about consequences fitting the crime. Essays are also a natural time-out. When you're thinking and writing, you can't be doing anything else.

Certainly you don't use the same discipline consequence

for everything. But having an everyday response for everyday misbehavior is smart discipline. Because another age-old law of discipline, which I made up in my old age, is this: A simple approach used well and long works far better than the most brilliant one used poorly and short.

Time-Out Time

Dear Dr. Ray,

What's an appropriate length of time for a preschooler to spend in time-out? I've read that one minute per year of age is a good rule of thumb.

The Timer

By "time-out," I'm assuming you mean to place your pre-schooler in a chair, corner, room, or on the steps, couch—some semi-isolated place for a period of time. In the old days, it was called going to your room, or sitting down, or visiting the corner. These days we've given it an air of psychological respectability: time-out.

Time-out has fostered many similar strategies: the quiet chair, thinking time, the cool-down rug, the sitting place. Whatever the name, it essentially means to remove little Harmony from one scene—where the action, fun, or trouble is—and place her in another—where it's quiet, boring, and trouble-free.

Some experts say that time-out is not punishment. Rather, it's a chance for a child to calm down and regroup. This can

In the old days, it was called going to your room, or sitting down, or visiting the corner. These days we've given it an air of psychological respectability: time-out.

be the effect, but I think we're playing semantics. We grown-ups may feel better by not thinking of time-out as punishment, but kids don't share our sentiment. What child will ask, "Excuse me, Mother. Do you mind if I sit in a chair with my back to the living room? I need to think a while."

Whether we mean it to be or not, time-out is boring. It is not something we want kids to want—not usually, anyway. That's what gives it its disciplinary or deterrent effect. Take a random sample of a hundred preschoolers, and I'd bet that all of them would rank time-out among their least favorite things in life, right down there with bedtime and siblings.

Because time-out is standard preschool discipline, parents wrestle with its length. How long is long enough to let the lesson settle in? The rule of one minute for each year in age is based on the developmental notion that little kids aren't readily capable of spending much time in any one place. Making little Patience stay put beyond a few minutes is pushing her past the limits of her attention span and endurance.

Like many theories of child rearing, this one is based on ideal circumstances. It probably would work pretty well with theoretical kids, but real ones eat it up. When given a time-out, what child says, "Of course, Mother, I'd love to go to the chair. Tell me how many minutes, and I'll set the timer to save you the trouble." Routinely, three-year-old Bliss hasn't even quieted down by the three-minute mark.

That kids so often verbally and physically resist time-out is further evidence that they don't see it as thinking time, but as punishment. Besides, what kind of discipline is it that enables a child to unload on us vocally for X minutes and then get up? Guess we showed him!

Here are guidelines that may make the one-minute-per-year rule more workable.

1. Insist on one *quiet* minute per year. Time does not begin until young Knight is silent. And time starts over if he starts over. In effect, Knight can shorten his time if he accepts it well.

Will this stress him beyond his developmental limits? First of all, Knight is passing time by acting up, so he's not completely bored. Second, there's nothing unhealthy about stretching your limits. In other words, Knight is learning to sit a little longer than he'd prefer to. That's what boring is all about. He's not going to be stunted emotionally because he had to stay in one place four minutes longer than he wanted or than an expert says he should have to.

2. Link the duration of the time-out to the seriousness of the infraction. Every parent has his or her own hierarchy of problem behavior. Toward the top are those things we personally find more serious, or those we want more quickly to teach our children not to do. For example, temper tantrums and sibling tormenting may top your list, while disrespect and rudeness may head another parent's. It only makes sense to link longer stays to more troublesome behaviors.

3. Make time-out boring. The more dull the location, the less time needed for Grace to simmer down. If she sits on a dining room chair with a panoramic view of family life, she can watch her surroundings to pass the time. If she stands somewhere with her back to the action, she'll have to be far more creative to avoid boredom. Then again, you might not want to test her creativity too much.

A caution: Every parent has to balance the need for supervision with the need for boredom. Sometimes it may just be better to keep Sigmund close by to avoid the trouble he could create behind your back.

One mother used her stairs creatively. Time-out on the first step was a five-minute stay. If her son talked, squawked, or walked while on the first step, he earned the second step, also worth five minutes. If quiet for five minutes on the second step, he could move to the first step. Five minutes of quiet there and he could leave. Last I heard, Mom was adding a fifth floor to her house.

Lots of Room

Dear Dr. Ray,

I've read that sending kids to their room is bad discipline because it's taking a special place and pairing it with punishment.

All Messed Up and No Place to Go

I'll do you one better. I've read that sending a child to his room can give him bad feelings toward sleep. But if that's so, since the days of early adolescence I should have been a complete insomniac.

Neither of these far-fetched warnings do I agree with in the least. To begin, a similar case could be made against nearly all discipline. If you make a teen write an essay on respect each time he's disrespectful, will he turn away from the English language? If you fine him a dollar, will he grow up hating money? Will a preschooler sent to a corner become corner-phobic? If he sits one too many times in time-out, will he develop an aversion to chairs?

Virtually every disciplinary consequence carries some negative component, or it wouldn't be disciplinary. It wouldn't teach a lesson or have a deterrent effect.

I suppose there are a few kids whose rooms could lose a little luster from their revisits, but even so, the pros of a time-out in their room far exceed the cons. Before getting into these, one condition needs to be set.

In a recent study of strong families, the most common discipline was room time, particularly for elementary schoolers and older.

Mickey's room must not be a branch of Disney World, complete with an eighteen-foot video screen, toy warehouse, and phone satellite linkup to nine countries. It should be a relatively quiet place with a bed, some books, and a few other comforts.

If not, you can a) thin it out or b) use another room. Many parents choose "b" because they can't afford to hire enough trucks to haul away the room's inventory.

A room stay is well suited to any number of daily misbehaviors: disrespect, sibling quibbling, temper surges, arguing.

Removal from the scene of the trouble is quick and effective. In a recent study of strong families, the most common discipline was room time, particularly for elementary schoolers and older.

A second benefit is the "out of your face" phenomenon. Rooms separate agitated, irritated, or instigated parties, be they parents and kids, kids and kids, or maybe parents and parents. As we noted in an earlier chapter, disciplinary turbulence is often not caused by the discipline itself but by the escalating words and emotions that can erupt during discipline. A firm room directive short-circuits trouble before it fuels itself. It allows both parties to simmer down more quickly, thus leaving much unsaid that is not meant and would later need explanation or apology. If you don't say it, it doesn't hurt.

A third benefit: Rooms give everyone time to think. Neither we nor little Fulbright may use the time for this purpose, but it's available. Some parents pair the room with a writing assignment to help a child better gather these thoughts. Be careful, however: You could be breeding a claustrophobic insomniac mislexic (hater of words).

Is it better for you or the child to determine the length of stay? That's your decision. Generally, consistency in using the room is more important than the particulars of time. If staying in the room is part of a house rule—for example, go to your room for a nasty tone of voice—then a specified time, say half an hour, probably will work better. It eliminates questions and looseness. And kids love looseness. It's a vehicle for debate.

Child-set time might be better when calm discussion is a goal: "Please think about this in your room and tell me when you're ready to talk," or "Settle down in your room until you're ready to apologize to your sister," or "Go to your room, and I'll be up when I'm calm."

Some other room ideas: Time starts over if Bedelia nags to come out, pitches a fit, or simply comes out. Time is doubled if she refuses to go to her room or has to be taken there.

Remember that the effectiveness of room time-out is directly related to your willingness to make it stick. One mother told me that if her son came out after a warning, he lost all privileges for the remainder of the day. Mom's attitude was: Quietly accept this reasonable consequence, or it'll only be much worse.

What is young Raddison allowed to do in his room? Again, that's up to you. But I would make off-limits the really neat stuff, such as phone, television, radio, toys. That leaves the quieter things such as sitting, thinking, sleeping, reading, fuming. All in all, still not a bad selection.

To Write Is Right

Dear Dr. Ray,

I've heard you advise requiring older children to write essays on their misconduct. I've also heard others say never to use writing as discipline.

Write Me Back

The reasoning against writing as a form of discipline is much like the reasoning we've noted against being sent to your room as a form of discipline: We want children to embrace the language and to find writing pleasurable. Therefore, we should never pair writing with something unpleasant, such as discipline. As we have seen, such logic doesn't hold up. Should children never be made to apologize for their actions for fear they will come to be repulsed by the act of apologizing, and ultimately by people themselves?

Anything used as a consequence to hold anyone accountable for his behavior is negative in the context it is used. It's supposed to be. It is teaching a lesson through repetition over time. That in no way means it will be viewed negatively in other contexts where it is freely chosen.

Besides, where are we getting this idea that writing is always supposed to be pleasurable? Most writers will tell you it's hard work. It's an act of the will, of self-discipline. The pleasure comes from the completion of the product. My favorite writing axiom is "If something is easy to read, it was likely hard to write."

Most writers will also tell you that to be a good writer, one element is crucial: practice. You become skilled by rewriting your rewriting. So you see, if you use essays, and young Webster acts up a lot, you could be raising his chances of someday winning a Pulitzer.

Let's even assume for a paragraph that essays do risk turning off kids toward writing. Even then, the benefits of essays far outweigh the risks.

First, essays teach children to gather their thoughts into a coherent whole. Edgar Allen communicates what he did, why it was wrong, what he could have done instead, how he can act better next time. In essence, he puts his developing conscience on paper.

Second, essays are revealing. They are windows into our children's minds, speaking of thoughts we may not hear out loud.

Third, essays are springboards to communication. My wife and I routinely talk over our children's essays with them. My wife also checks all grammar and spelling, requiring corrections. It's surprising how fast the kids' language skills are rising.

Fourth, essays are tailor-made for routine problems: back talk, sibling squabbling, chore shirking, disorderly conduct in public. Talk about making the response logically follow the crime. Few disciplinary consequences do this for a wider range of behavior than essays.

Essays are revealing. They are windows into our children's minds, speaking of thoughts we may not hear out loud.

Fifth, essays are easy for parents to use. We don't have to rack our brains for how to respond if we've already established, say, that disrespectful tone automatically leads to a three-hundred-word essay on "mouth control." And an essay is quantifiable. It may begin at three hundred, but as young Oxford debates your decision, it rises to three hundred fifty, then four hundred, then five hundred.

This escalating discipline not only restrains you from arguing in return; it teaches Oxford about your resolve in the face of escalating nastiness. One suggestion: Put a cap on your numbers. Otherwise, after the fifty-fourth verbal comeback, you could hear yourself ranting, "Two billion!"

How do you ensure that the essay is done now and not at the turn of the century? One good house rule might be this: "All privileges cease until the essay is complete."

My wife and I have relied quite a bit on assigning these compositions to our children. When they are just beginning to write (age five or six), we have them copy essays (twenty-five to fifty words) already composed by us. The preschoolers laughed, but their day was not long in coming.

Like much of parenting, what we intend in discipline isn't always what happens. My son learned early the "reiterating writing" technique. He would pen: "And you should not do that because God will not like it and Jesus will not like it and the angels will not like it and Mom will not like it and Dad will not like it and ..." We were forced to add some composition guidelines.

Sometimes, just the humor is worth it. Once after acting up, in the waiting room of my office no less, my son wrote an essay containing the line, "And if you act bad, people will not think your dad is a good sicolojist [sic] and they won't want to hear him talk and we won't have money to pay our bills, or eat, or have a house, and I won't get to play baseball either."

Just think: From one episode of misbehavior, he had us homeless. Talk about conscience run wild. After I had used this example in a presentation to parents, and my son was in the audience, all future essays contained a "P.S.: Dad, don't use this in your talks, OK?"

I told Andrew I wouldn't use it in my talks. But I didn't say anything about this book.

Rules of the House

Dear Dr. Ray,

My wife and I don't always agree on how to discipline our son and daughter, ages ten and six. She says I can be too hard on them. I think she gives in too much.

Disunited Front

No two parents will ever raise a child identically. No two personalities (and hence factors such as reactivity, tolerance level, and consistency) are the same. Further, parenting involves on-the-spot judgment as well as an overall philosophy. It is far too encompassing for complete accord.

That parents are not always of one mind is not in itself an obstacle to consistency. Trouble comes when disagreement leads to undercutting each other, especially within range of juvenile eyes and ears. Agreeing to disagree later and finding some compromise works well to bring parents together over the long run. When both parties at least listen to the other's view, eventually most differences get smoothed out enough to unite the front.

A more immediate path to reduced disciplinary discord is through house rules. These are simple expectations backed by simple consequences. For maximum success, a house rule needs several features.

First and foremost, parents must agree on it. Without mutual support, a house rule merely becomes another point of child rearing contention.

Second, a house rule involves a recurrent (weekly, daily,

hourly, minutely) trouble spot: back talk, sibling quibbling, chore shirking, temper tempests. It is best used for the most irritating stuff.

Third, house rule consequences are automatic. They result when the rule is broken, without nagging ("I'm telling you one last time, Butkus, I don't want to have to call in our rule"), rereminding ("What did I say was the new rule? Do you remember? Do you want me to write it on your arm?"), and threatening ("OK, break the rule one more time. See what happens. See if I don't triple it.") Let your consequences do your talking.

> The good Lord gave the whole world ten core rules. A house is a much smaller place.

Finally, try to keep your rules to a manageable number. The good Lord gave the whole world ten core rules. A house is a much smaller place.

House rules provide the common ground upon which you and your spouse can stand. With agreed-upon consequences in place, neither of you has to judge what to do each and every time the kids act up. Besides making expectations more clear for the kids, rules make discipline less open-ended for parents.

Here is a sampler of house rules.

- *You hit, you sit.* No physical contact with a sibling without his or her permission. Cost is X minutes sitting time. For mutual squabbling, both children sit at the table. No talking allowed. Neither can get up until each gives the other permission to get up.
- *You fight, you write.* For use with older siblings, both parties write 150-word apologies to the other.
- *You talk back, you walk back* or *You get mean, you leave the*

scene. Back talk leads to an immediate half an hour in room, if logistics permit. If not, delay the room stay until possible. Time doesn't count unless it's quiet. For older children, add a two-hundred-word report on a topic of their choice from the encyclopedia. Who knows? Someday they could become *Jeopardy* champions.

- *Pick up or pay up.* Every toy Mom or Dad has to pick up goes in their box (bag, closet, warehouse) for one week. One dime fee for return.

- *You shirk, you work.* If you neglect doing your household chore on time, privileges are unavailable until that chore, and an additional one, is complete.

Rules are a kind form of discipline for all parties. For kids, they quietly lay out expectations. Fewer arguments, harsh words, and hurt feelings ensue when guidelines are clear. For parents, rules bring peace. When in place prior to trouble, they are a means to disciplinary harmony and thus a genuinely united front.

Blackout

Dear Dr. Ray,

How can I get my children (ages five, ten, and twelve) to accept discipline quietly and willingly?

Battle-Fatigued

"Quietly" is an easier goal than "willingly." Willingness doesn't consistently happen until childhood is well past, and even then, lots of grown-ups don't take any kind of discipline well.

Your question is a broad one, but most parents who ask it mean this: How can I get my kids to accept their consequences (whatever they might be) without an argument, resistance, or even an all-out battle? Indeed, making discipline stick is the number one disciplinary struggle for most parents today.

All kids misbehave; most do so lots. But when that misbehavior directly challenges your authority, it dramatically raises the child rearing stakes. In words or deeds, it says: "I will not accept your legitimate right to discipline me as you see fit. I will nag, argue, plead, scream, fight—in short, whatever—to escape consequences, create chaos, or punish you back."

Such conduct may be born of spontaneous emotions, willful resistance, or any combination along the continuum. No matter. You must respond to it firmly and uncompromisingly, lest it become a pattern that, with years, will grow only more intense.

Let's say you've just explained to your twelve-year-old son a new house rule: Any form of disrespect to anyone will result in a minimum four-hundred-word essay on respect. Whereupon he gives you that adolescent look of disdain that says, "Is that what you learned from your parenting books?" Implication: "You're not smart enough to come up with this one on your own."

Clearly he's earned his first four hundred words. Clearly also, this is just the beginning of a conflict—a conflict that could get long, intense, and ugly. So what do you do? As the parent, you have many options. (I know, you just wish you could think of them fast enough.)

The response I've found to be by far the most effective is "blackout." Blackout is the immediate and complete shutdown of all benefits and privileges, except for love, food, water, and—OK—the bathroom.

Your son has no grasp of what you control—electrical outlets, utilities, laundry service, food service, transportation, money supply, the airwaves, computer chips, all links to the outside world.

Blackout is the immediate and complete shutdown of all benefits and privileges, except for love, food, water, and—OK—the bathroom.

If he has soccer practice tonight, he'd best call his coach and explain why he won't be there. Your transportation is parked until you get the essay.

If the family has planned to eat out, your son comes along, but he can't order. He can eat at home; restaurants are privileges.

If a friend calls, the call is yours to take, not his.

In essence, until you receive a thoughtful essay—or whatever consequence you levy—all "entitlements" become privileges to be regained by cooperation.

Similarly, suppose your five-year-old simply will not go quietly to the corner when you ask him to. Or, once there, he comes out twenty-seven times, screams for seventeen minutes, or runs up to his room and trashes it. You know the routine. Although it varies some from child to child, the overall resistance pattern is pretty standard.

Well, argue no more about the corner. Blackout is in force. If Will plays with a toy, it's taken until corner time is served, which is now doubled because of his initial resistance. If he asks to watch "Walter the Wonder Whale," your response could be, "Oh, no, Honey, no Walter. You need to go to the corner first." If you go to Grandma's, and his cousins are there, "Will, you know you can play as soon as you give me all your corner time." If you're especially brazen, you can tell Grandma, "No, thanks, Mom, he can't have any ice cream. Not until he pays his corner time."

Is blackout mean? Is it a hardhearted, dictatorial squashing of a child's spirit? Certainly you can be mean about it, as you can with any discipline. But ultimately, blackout is very kind.

One, it teaches an invaluable lesson: I am your mother (or father), and I love you too much to allow you to be nasty and defiant.

Two, it short-circuits conflict. You will no longer battle. No more will you nag, argue, threaten, plead, or fight. Sound familiar? That's how kids act.

Instead, you will quietly and confidently take charge of the situation. As one mom put it, "I don't have to get into ugly mouth-to-mouth combat. I have tanks behind me."

Three, blackout leads to more family peace and goodwill. When kids accept their consequences, discipline is over much more quickly. Life returns to normal in minutes instead of hours.

One final word. Don't let any expert tell you that blackout is a power struggle. It's the exact opposite. A power struggle occurs when a parent drops to a kid's level and fights it out with childish weapons. Blackout is a refusal to fight. It sends a powerful, silent statement: I'm the parent, and I love you way too much to let you, and me, act this way.

Spare or Spoil?

Dear Dr. Ray,

What is your opinion about spanking? I personally don't see anything wrong with it, but so many experts and even parents are against it that I'm confused.

Bottom Line

Spanking—the most controversial form of discipline. What was once considered standard, even healthy, practice has increasingly come under the experts' critical microscope. Spanking has been assailed on several fronts: It's ineffective, some claim, and only breeds resentment; it teaches children to be aggressive; it sends mixed messages; and most ominously, it is a form of child abuse.

Is spanking really guilty of all this psychological evil, or is spanking still a legitimate disciplinary option that can be used effectively by loving parents?

What is spanking? Old-style spanking—the semiritualized hairbrush on the bottom or switch to the legs—isn't practiced much anymore. When parents today talk spanking, they typically mean a hand swat or two on the legs, backside, or hand at the time of infraction. This will be our definition of spanking, though some parents do insist that their ruler and wooden spoon aren't just for measuring and cooking.

Let's examine the indictments against spanking, one at a time.

1. *Spanking is ineffective and only breeds resentment.* To be sure, spanking is not 100 percent effective. No discipline is, or even comes close.

So why does spanking sometimes seem so futile? First, parents understandably don't like to spank; they'd rather do almost anything else first. So—consciously or unconsciously—we make spanking a "last resort" discipline.

Spike has been unruly, defiant, and generally obnoxious for the past twenty-seven minutes. After nagging, overreasoning, and threatening, mostly to no avail, in exasperation we swat. By this time, he's agitated, we're agitated, the dog's agitated, the neighbors are agitated, and the swat is more a show of frustration than a deliberate attempt to teach something.

Then, too, because spanking bothers us, we stay our hand. That is, we go through the motion of a swat, which effectively only evokes a look from little Conan that says, "You wrinkled my sweatpants." To have any chance to work, a swat must be felt. It must make its presence clearly known. Otherwise, it's not spanking. It's nonverbal nagging. And kids are too savvy and determined to pay any heed to paper discipline.

> To have any chance to work, a swat must be felt. Otherwise, it's not spanking. It's nonverbal nagging.

Can spanking cause resentment? Sure, sometimes. So can any discipline, depending upon how it's carried out. Even the purest of discipline—done with love, calm, and firmness—can trigger some resentment, because kids don't generally agree with, appreciate, or like discipline when it's happening. Further, if everybody is already agitated when the spanking comes, inflamed emotions get more so. "Spanking is ineffective" oftentimes really means "ineffective spanking."

2. *Spanking teaches aggression. It teaches force as a way to solve problems.* Aggression is a highly complex phenomenon. It is affected by genetics, temperament, social surroundings, and opportunity, to name only a few variables. To say that an occasional spank alone teaches aggression is extremely simplistic and psychologically absurd. It's tantamount to predicting that a child who is raised by loving, moral parents will learn immorality because she occasionally hears her parents curse.

One of the strongest rebuttals to the "spanking teaches aggression" notion comes from a recent nationwide study of strong families. One hundred families, nominated by national state teachers of the year as the best families they had ever seen, were interviewed to learn the elements of their success.

Did they spank? Seventy percent said yes. Spanking had been one of their disciplinary options when their children were younger.

Nearly four hundred youngsters were included in these families. They were described by their teachers as mature, caring, responsible, moral, and of high character. Terms such as "aggressive" or anything remotely similar were never used.

I can cite no better piece of real life "proof" that when done in the context of a loving home, spanking breeds neither psychological trouble nor aggression. In fact, for most of these successful parents, a well-timed and well-placed swat saved many more problems than it ever caused.

3. *Spanking sends mixed messages.* In other words, if you don't allow a child to hit, kick, bite, pinch others, yet you yourself "hit" him, you are confusing him. You are disciplining his aggression with your aggression. On the surface, this sounds somewhat reasonable. But a deeper look will show its fallacy.

When a young child assails someone, it's usually spontaneous and with ill intent. He's upset, or retaliating, or trying to intimidate. It's an aggressive move. Any good result coming of it will be accidental. On the other hand, effective spanking is deliberate and well intentioned; it aims to instruct.

If Angel bites Bruno, you could sit her in a chair for punishment. After thirty or forty sittings, she may cease. In the meantime, Bruno collects teeth marks. A stinging swat, however, may much more quickly teach Angel to keep her teeth in her mouth while at the same time protecting Bruno.

Will Angel be confused by your physical action to prohibit hers? Most likely she's not even capable of such sophisticated misreasoning. And if she is, that's OK. With maturity, someday she'll better understand the crucial difference between what you did and what she did. In the meantime she'll be less aggressive toward Bruno.

4. *Spanking is child abuse.* This is the most ludicrous charge of all. Spanking and child abuse are not even on the same continuum.

True, abuse often includes hitting. But it's not spanking; it's an attack. It's no attempt to deter trouble or teach. It's a lashing out with a vengeance.

Abuse is cruelty. Spanking is legitimate discipline. It is

moderation tempered by good judgment. To equate spanking with child abuse is to heap guilt of the worst kind on loving parents.

All this is not my attempt to promote spanking as a means of discipline in your home. To spank or not must be your decision. If you choose not to spank, plenty of other alternatives are available.

My argument is against those who flat-out indict spanking as child rearing sin and parents who spank as guilty and incompetent. Spanking, I believe, deserves to be judged as all discipline is judged: How well is this working, for you, for your child, and within the values and behaviors you're trying to instill.

Discipline Delegating

Dear Dr. Ray,

What is your opinion on giving kids a say in the consequences for certain misbehavior?

Consulting Parent

Some parents believe there's a time and place for kids to set their own disciplinary consequences: The time is when they're twenty-seven, and the place is their own apartment, maybe somewhere in Europe. In fact, however, I think that allowing youngsters' input into at least some of their discipline is fraught with advantages.

First, kids sometimes confront us with such bizarre stunts

that we're too shell-shocked to think clearly. We can't discern any possible rationale for their behavior, much less decide what to do about it.

One source of ideas is the source of the trouble: "Iris, I'm not quite sure what to do about this. I've never had someone step on every petunia in my flower box looking for a nerf ball. You tell me what I should do."

Often you'll hear, "I don't know." Kids never know anything when it concerns them. Nonetheless, you can help Iris gain some insight by following with "Well, if you don't decide, I'll have to. Give me something reasonable, and I'll go with it." Iris may take a shot at being reasonable, especially if she thinks it will help her escape our "unreasonable" discipline.

A second advantage to concocting their own disciplinary consequences (an adolescent referred to this as "picking your poison") is that the children may be more cooperative in seeing them through. Armstrong may more quietly shovel the snow by himself next time as his price for hitting his brother in the head with an ice ball this time. After all, he publicly picked that outcome. You have it on record with a copy at your attorney's office.

Third, discipline delegating gives Buford a chance to ponder. In thinking about fair consequences, he is also thinking about the nature of his act. If he needs time to reflect, he can retreat to his room or a similarly quiet, cluttered place and later return with an answer or two. A few youngsters will actually provide several options. These are the ones destined to be counselor types.

Finally, you have the last word on all joint venture discipline. Leave the matter completely up to Spike, and you could easily hear the likes of "OK, I'll write, 'I'm sorry' twice ... you got any carbon paper?" If given enough time—anywhere between a minute and six years—most kids will conjure up a legitimate outcome: "I think I should pay for all new petunias with my allowance, and not have any TV until I do."

Then, too, kids can be harder on themselves than we would ever be: "I think I should write, 'I am very, very, very, very sorry for totally destroying all our flowers and making our home the ugliest house in the neighborhood so nobody will ever come and visit us and I'll grow up having to go to encounter groups every day before work.' I should write that a million times. And I think I should pay for the broken petunias by mowing the lawn at a penny an acre ... with the weed eater."

> Leave the matter completely up to Spike, and you could easily hear the likes of "OK, I'll write, 'I'm sorry' twice ... you got any carbon paper?"

You may have to temper Chastity's self-discipline while adding a little meat to Spike's. In the end, asking kids for discipline help can spur thoughtful answers, teach a good lesson, and keep you from getting an ulcer struggling to think up something appropriate.

SIX

Discipline and the Nature of Kids

A ll discipline interacts with a most unpredictable and unique force: the individual child. Some kids can be disciplined with a look, even a glance. Others require a battalion of tanks to keep them somewhat in line. The success of any disciplinary approach depends heavily upon the inborn personality of the child toward whom it is directed. For that reason, understanding some core truths about personality can help you better know what to expect when you do have to discipline.

No End in Sight

Dear Dr. Ray,
Do children ever stop misbehaving?

Weary

Some questions are elegantly simple, yet profound. They seek the very essence of a truth. No, children never stop misbehaving. Adults never stop misbehaving. Nobody ever stops misbehaving.

Parents instinctively know this. We just as instinctively tend to deny it. Almost unconsciously we hope, even expect, that misconduct will someday be all gone. True, lots of kid turbulence—

temper tempests, meal ordeals, bedtime bad times, tattling—does fade away with the years. But the core nature of misbehavior—defiance, passive resistance, unruliness, irresponsibility—will take many forms over a childhood, and will never completely disappear.

A fourteen-year-old may not fling herself to the floor, slapping her head with each sob, but any parent confronting a hostile or disdainful teen can tell you the most nasty forms of temper aren't always the loudest or most theatrical. The rebellion of a toddler may be more in your face and space than that of a twelve-year-old's subtle foot dragging. Yet the older child may be acting no less willfully.

Children never stop misbehaving. Adults never stop misbehaving. Nobody ever stops misbehaving.

Is this to say that discipline really only serves to eradicate one misbehavior until another evolves to take its place? Absolutely not. The purpose of discipline is to teach good behavior. As such, the better the discipline, the better the behavior over time. But—and this is a big but—discipline will remain an integral part of your parenthood until the day young Harmony leaves the house.

Most misconduct exhibits a similar life cycle. The behavior appears for the first time at some point in development. The longer it lingers, the longer it will take for discipline, no matter how firm and consistent, to reduce it. Initially its intensity may surge in response to discipline. But as the discipline brakes are applied, the misconduct slows, sometimes dramatically to a near zero level.

Seldom, however, is the misbehavior ever fully eradicated.

Why? Because kids are human (most of the time) and humans, until the day they leave this earth, retain the proclivity to act wrongly.

Let's say you've decided to assign a five-hundred-word essay on respect each and every time your fifteen-year-old gets mouthy. Within mere weeks his snotty attitude is one tenth of its former strength. Yet that last stubborn, residual one tenth may persevere until the day he moves out.

This doesn't mean your discipline isn't working. It's working very well. It took care of 90 percent of the problem. As you persevere in disciplining that remaining 10 percent, tell yourself that you are teaching your son that disrespect is wrong, and that he will always be held accountable for it, even if he doesn't learn your lesson completely. Time and life are on your side. They should take care of most of that last 10 percent.

Take heart. The bad news is that you'll never see perfect results. The good news is that you can get real close. Besides, there have to be some things for their spouses to work on.

The Second-Most-Powerful Factor

Dear Dr. Ray,

I have three children, ages five, nine, and ten. I've tried to raise them all the same, yet they are so different. How can such distinct personalities come from the same parents?

One Mom

113

Parenting determines much of how a child matures. But it is by no means the only influence. Unfortunately, the factors that get the most press are among the weakest, and the factor that is least often talked about is among the strongest.

Birth order gets singled out as a potent molder of personality. The fact is that birth order exerts a very weak effect, if any, upon children. The only research in this area with any consistent support involves firstborns. As a group they are slightly more independent and achieving.

This trait, however, may come more from natural parenting changes than from Prima's position in the family. With the first child, we sterilize everything within fifteen feet of her. By the time the last one rolls around, we throw him a big dirt ball and say, "Here, chew on this awhile." With experience our style changes. We tend to become more easygoing.

What is the one factor that, next to you, most influences a child's behavior? Temperament—the way God wires each child.

Neither does diet impact behavior anywhere near as much as some would have you believe. Not even sugar. Some theories can almost convince you that if you just fed Cookie a tomato sandwich with twelve bean sprouts and tofu, he'd do better in math.

Parenting should be so straightforward. Again, the better the research, the less the connection between diet and behavior. Changes in Cookie's behavior seem to come primarily from our expectations and attention.

What is the one factor that, next to you, most influences a child's behavior? Temperament—the way God wires each child.

Chastity enters the world with a gentleness that seems to say, "Oh, hello, Mother. Did you want me to sleep through the night on the first night home from the hospital or the second?" Spike is born with a vengeance that prompts the pediatrician to give you his home phone number.

Look crosswise at Chastity and she crumbles to the floor, cries herself to sleep, and doesn't misbehave for the next two weeks, every night leaving love notes with hearts around the edges on your pillow. To get Spike to sit on a chair, you have to glue his hands to the wall behind him. He chews them off at the wrist to get out. That is his nature, the kind of kid he is. He's stubborn, or active, or spacey, or impulsive, or immature.

I've noticed something else. There are a lot of Spikettes floating around, too. I think it has something to do with ERA or PMS or one of those letter things.

If you're raising a Spike, and your sister is raising a Chastity—or the male counterpart, Oxford—you both might be using identical discipline: same words, same tone of voice, same consequences, same consistency. Yet at the end of three months, she'll say, "I haven't seen the problem for eleven weeks," and you'll say, "I don't think he's done it for the past hour, but I'm not sure; he's with his grandmother."

Children's individual natures are inextricably tied to everything—how they mature, how you discipline them, how they relate to others, how they see the world. That individual nature is ever present, and a wise parent respects its power, or learns to.

One closing thought. Don't you have to stifle yourself around parents of Chastitys? Sometimes they can be so smug.

The child is practically raising herself. She's been sitting at the birthday party and hasn't moved for three solid hours. She doesn't want to wrinkle her dress.

Meanwhile, Spike has already stepped in the cake and bit the cat. You can see Chastity's mother thinking, "My child would not even entertain that kind of behavior." And you're thinking, "That's 'cause your child's a sissy. Do you want to spend nine minutes in one room with Spike and see who crawls out?"

The Flesh Is Willful

Dear Dr. Ray,

Is it my imagination, or are there more "strong-willed" children than there used to be?

Willing to Listen

Once I asked a group of parents, "How many of you have a Spike or Spikette (a.k.a. Damien, Chuckie, or Christine—if you remember the movies)?" The great majority of parents raised a hand. Indeed, most parents think they have at least one real challenge, sometimes more.

Let's ponder the implications. If most moms and dads think they have a strong-willed child, what does that say about kids in general, or about their parents? One, the typical child is strong-willed. Or two, parents are less strong-willed than kids. Personally, I see both realities at play.

By the way, the term "strong-willed" has a lot of relatives:

"stubborn," "relentless," "determined," "mind of her own," "iron-willed," and my favorite, "difficult child." (This last one is redundant.)

Consider the basic baby. Twenty inches long or so. Seven pounds. Main abilities are crying, fussing, leaking out of body orifices. No morals, no socialization, no delay of gratification.

In her mind, she is the center of the universe. If she doesn't get what she wants the instant she wants it, she becomes a raving emotional lunatic.

Is this strong-willed? It depends upon your definition. But one thing seems clear. This child is not about to cooperate with us.

To gauge the willfulness of your child, take a simple test. Have you ever heard the likes of "Your little Rex is no problem at all; he's one of Stormy's nicest friends." or "He was fine until you walked in." or "He's a delight in class. I wish I had a whole room of kids just like him."

Upon hearing this last one, you pull out your wallet picture of Rex, show it in disbelief to the teacher, saying, "No, I'm here for the Miller boy. He's a little brown-haired kid with a gap in his teeth. What school is this and who are you?"

If you hear any of these things, you don't have a real Spike or Spikette. You have a child perfectly capable of more cooperation and self-control than you are being shown at home.

Sometimes I will tease my clients. "Do you think your child is strong-willed?"

"Oh," they insist, "absolutely, will of iron, oppositional, relentless."

"What's the school say?"

"You know, I don't understand it," they often reply. "The school doesn't see any of this."

"If he's so strong-willed," I ask, "how do you explain how the teacher, with a fraction of your authority, can control him along with nineteen others for several hours?"

Usually I get some version of "Do you think he holds it in all day, and when he gets home he has to explode?"

Tough little people, when socialized, make for strong big people.

"No," I answer, "I think he knows where the speed limit is twenty and where it's the autobahn."

All this is not to say that kids don't vary widely in their strength of will. Of my ten children, a few I can raise by clearing my throat (Angel and Earnest). A few I need to carry a bazooka just to remind them who's in charge (Butkus and Conan). Most are somewhere in between. But I don't consider any of the ten unconquerably strong-willed.

How can this be? Simple. Their mother is stronger-willed. So even when they are at their relentless worst, ultimately she will prevail. And God willing, their intense personality will over years be channeled and tempered into a force for good. Tough little people, when socialized, make for strong big people.

God has a great sense of humor. Sometimes he gives a Chastity or an Oxford to parents first. Then we get cocky. We think we must be naturals at this child rearing stuff. We have none of the turmoil our mere mortal fellow parents experience.

Then comes Bruno. I call this the shell-shocked second child syndrome. The first child was not normal. The second child is. Our first one was a freebie, a mulligan from God. He said, "Here, play with this; I'll save the real kid for later."

Balancing the Discipline Scale

Dear Dr. Ray,

My nine-year-old son brings much more discipline upon himself than does his seven-year-old sister, who is more cooperative by nature. He accuses us of being unfair and liking her more. Any way I can make him see we're not playing favorites?

Likes Me Less

Here are three options:

One, overlook much of your son's misconduct so that you discipline both children equally.

Two, discipline your daughter for nitpicky kid stuff so she gets more discipline than she deserves.

Three, try to make your son understand that you discipline only when it's called for, and since he calls for it more, he receives it more. Discipline has nothing to do with favoritism or who it is you like more. Repeat this truth regularly until he accepts it.

I'll bet you think I'm going to recommend option three. Actually, none of them is very good. Three is the route most parents take, with unending frustration, because little Justice will seldom acknowledge his role in your differential discipline, no matter how eloquent and flawless your reasoning.

Have you yet heard, "Mother, I've been so stubborn. Of course, you don't like me less. I realize that I am fully responsible for the consequences I'm bringing upon myself, and that if I acted more like Chastity, I too would rarely be disciplined. In fact, I think I'm going to study her behavior and see just what it is that makes her so pleasant and mature." Kids don't like to let little things like reality and logic cloud their view of discipline.

Actually, options one and two aren't as far-fetched as they sound. Many parents feel compelled to balance the discipline scale by easing up on Butkus or cracking down on Chastity. One mom put it this

Kids don't like to let little things like reality and logic cloud their view of discipline.

way: "If I disciplined him whenever he deserved it, he'd get disciplined ten times as much as his sister. As it is, I let him get away with about half of his nastiness, and he still gets disciplined five times as much."

Ultimately, either option is unfair to the child who behaves better. Why should he or she be held to separate, more rigorous standards just because a sibling is unjustly crying "foul"?

Are there options other than the above? Yes, or else I would have written myself into a corner.

To begin, I recommend that you mete out discipline as it is deserved, independently of what a child thinks. A truth of family life is that no two children require equal amounts of guidance and firmness.

Second, quit defending yourself to Justice. He's determined not to agree with or accept the facts. You'll only get dragged into protracted arguments, which will likely convince him further that he has a legitimate gripe. After all, why would you spend so much time trying to talk him out of his perception?

Third, and most important, be extra attentive to Justice in between discipline episodes. Rather than struggling to make everything even between him and his sister, balance his discipline with increased affection and attention. Put another way, instead of disciplining him less, you'll be loving up on him more.

Will Justice come to realize your true fairness? Probably not for a while. Over time, though, he'll misbehave less. And then his discipline will be more, or should I say less, like Chastity's.

One other thing. The teen years are coming, and they can alter the whole parenting landscape. Sometimes the docile child flares up and the feisty one mellows out. There, now; don't you feel better?

The Terrible Whats?

Dear Dr. Ray,

My twin sons are twenty months old and thoroughly enjoyable. Everyone is warning me that the terrible twos are just around the corner. I'm getting nervous.

Terrible Twos Times Two

The terrible twos, in my opinion, are close to being a developmental myth. There are a few bits of truth to the notion, but there is much psychological junk. Yes, somewhere in the general vicinity of this age, most little ones make a quantum leap in willfulness, embrace "no" as 57 percent of their vocabulary, and start to assert their way of doing things as superior to yours. It is not so, however, that the twos (plus or minus one year) are an unavoidably ugly phase to be weathered on the way to calmer developmental waters.

First, by temperament some kids never become a terrible two. They are naturally cooperative or docile, and the twos present nothing more terrible than some sporadic bouts of feistiness. The fact that little Harmony never enters a real challenging stage is not—as one well-known expert implies—evidence of psychological stunting that could manifest itself someday at age seventeen in an emotional misfit. It is evidence, rather, of her overall sweet nature, at two, ten, or twenty.

Sixteen is the terrible twos times eight plus a driver's license.

Second, some children enter the terrible twos at eighteen months and some at three years. Many are the parents who thought they passed through the terrible twos pretty much unscathed only to be shell-shocked by the fiery fours. My wife (who is raising ten children, eleven counting me) maintains that peak preschool brattiness in her book emerges well after two. Compared to the calculated opposition of a three- or four-year-old, the twos were relatively benign.

Third, every age of childhood has its own particular phases, problems, and patterns. The twos are not unique in this sense. In fact, if you're looking for something to get nervous about, the complexity of later ages makes the twos look like a developmental piece of cake.

Our youngest, Elizabeth, just turned three. And I learned never to say, "Lizzie is in her terrible twos." Because if I was talking to a parent of teenagers, I could easily hear something like, "What's the matter? She won't eat her carrots? My son wants purple hair with a ring through his nose!" As someone once put it, "Sixteen is the terrible twos times eight plus a driver's license."

So how nervous should you be about what is heading your way in the next year or so with your sons? Not much. They may not pass through anything "terrible"—such as temper tempests or bedtime bad times—until they're four. So why fret now?

Then again, maybe these adorable cherubs will start to believe as soon as next week that they know more about life than you do and will start to challenge your heretofore acceptable limits and rules. That's OK. It's real parenthood time. If you deal with your son's newfound stubborn streak, unruliness, or whatever, it most likely won't mushroom into worse stuff with the years. Most of it will pass, though some of it will evolve into different, more sophisticatedly rowdy kidhood.

Sometimes parents will say things like "She's never thrown such an intense fit before." And sometimes I'll respond, "Has she ever been five before?" Or "This is the first time he's ever looked straight in my face and lied to me." Has he ever been twelve before?

In summary, there's good news, bad news, and then more good news. The first good news: The terrible twos aren't really so terrible. They only mark the start of childish assertiveness.

The bad news: Once you pass through the terrible twos, it doesn't get easier. Each age presents new challenges, usually more complex with the years.

But good news wins out in the end: The more willing you are to handle the terrible whatevers, the more terrifics you'll have, now and later.

Life's a Stage

Dear Dr. Ray,

My three-year-old has really gotten difficult in the past few months. My friend says it's only a stage, and it'll pass. Will it?

Waiting

Maybe it will. Maybe it won't. I'm sorry; I never used to talk like that. It all started when I became a psychologist.

Maybe it will pass. Childhood is full of all kinds of behavioral comings and goings. Much misconduct starts up mysteriously, out of nowhere. It lingers awhile, makes your life tough, and then passes. You didn't really do anything to cause it to arrive, and you really didn't do much to cause it to leave. It seemed to possess a life of its own.

Some examples of this problem? The relentless "no-ing" of a two-year-old. The falling down fits of a three-year-old. The tattling of a six-year-old, the moodiness of a twelve-year-old, or the "atti-tone" of a thirteen-year-old.

Age brings with it new conduct, some good, some bad. All throughout parenthood, you are forced to face, and face down, all kinds of behavior that never before was part of your child's way, or demeanor, or arsenal. You could say that with maturity come new forms of immaturity.

Time does indeed seem to cure some share of misbehavior. The problem is, you can't know for sure what will go away on its own and what won't. Time can be a parent's ally or foe, depending.

Maybe it won't pass. While much misconduct can crop up

initially as a stage, if left untreated, it can endure, and even fester into other stuff far more intense than the original phase. Let's say your little one's defiance is accompanied by fits. If you don't discipline the fits now, they may become a habit growing more nasty as Will becomes older, bigger, stronger, smarter, and slicker. In essence, the terrible twos can become the thundering threes can become the fiery fours can become ...

Any form of misbehavior is much more likely to pass eventually if you deal with it and discipline it. On the one hand, your friend may be right when she says, "It's just a stage." On the other hand, she could be quite wrong when she predicts it will pass.

Many are the behaviors that came to stay because the parent waited for them to subside with the passing of the stage.

The main predictor of whether a behavior passes or not is you. If you stand by passively, hoping your child will outgrow his or her defiance, your patience might be rewarded. But it's not likely. Over time bad behavior tends to fuel itself unless it is corrected. Many are the behaviors that came to stay because the parent waited for them to subside with the passing of the stage.

Often, too, behavior may go through phases in form but not substance. For example, a fit for a three-year-old involves writhing, flailing, and leaking from facial orifices. A fit from an eight-year-old involves yelling, slamming, and environmental assault. A fit from a fourteen-year-old involves, well, let's not talk about it. The tantrum itself has evolved (gone through stages, if you will), but the underlying problem—giving way to outbursts when frustrated—is still around.

So tell your friend you are committed to proving her right.

Your parental will and firmness will ensure that your child is just going through a stage, and indeed it will soon pass.

The Look of Discipline

Dear Dr. Ray,

Why do my kids routinely ignore me when I tell them to do something but all their father has to do is look and they jump?

Feeling Bad

Don't feel too bad. Few children respond identically to both parents. Just as no two kids are exactly alike, no two parents are exactly alike. You and your spouse probably differ in many ways—warmth, talkativeness, patience, consistency. Therefore, your kids' selective oblivion toward you is most likely nothing personal, but more a reflection of the dynamics of your interaction.

That last phrase was a bit shrinky sounding, so let me talk English.

Your lament is common. Typically a child does respond better to one parent's discipline than the other's. In your house, it's Dad's, so let's consider why, starting with the little ones.

Preschoolers as a group seem to react more cooperatively to fathers than to mothers. In no way does this imply that moms are less skilled disciplinarians. There are other influences. Dads have deeper, stronger voices. They tend to be more imposing, more commanding of attention, at least to eyes three feet off the ground.

Of course, this image effect usually wears off with time. Kids get bigger, more accustomed to Dad, and they'll learn to tune him out if he practices only gorilla discipline.

Gorillas can look extremely intimidating. They puff themselves up, beat their chests, growl, but it's mostly show unless they're threatened. While dads may enter the discipline arena with a slight physical advantage, if they don't actually learn to discipline, children will eventually ignore their bluster. Kids are far too fearless to be intimidated by someone only twice their size.

Kids are far too fearless to be intimidated by someone only twice their size.

There's another reason Dad may get more cooperation. Though not always, in general, children push harder on the parent they are around more. For kids, familiarity doesn't breed contempt; it breeds knowledge. And they will use that knowledge to probe for all our weak spots, guilt nerves, and inconsistencies. They want to get from point A to point B, and you're in the way. So if they can't go through you, they'll go around you, and ignore you if they have to.

What's the upshot of all this? The more time you spend around Les, the harder you must work to be consistent in your discipline, and to follow words with action instead of more words.

You would also be wise to look for differences between your and your husband's disciplinary styles. Is he more consistent than you? Does he speak calmly but with resolve? If his "look" fails to get cooperation, will there be consequences?

My father's first-line discipline was a resounding *"Hey!"* That usually got my attention. It wasn't the "hey" that made me move, but my certainty that something more tangible would follow if I ignored the word.

Indeed, many parents recall, "All my mother had to do was give me the evil eye." "My father would just look at us over his glasses." "My mom only had to snap her fingers and we knew."

How did our parents exert this quiet authority? They worked at it. There's no magic in looks, glasses, or fingers. It was their willingness to back up those warning signals with concrete, sure action if necessary. Pretty soon just the gestures were sufficient.

If after all this self-analyzing, you conclude that there are few discipline differences between you and your husband, then my speculation is simply that the kids are pushing harder on you because they know your style and your soft spots. The good news is that you can, with a little self-work, change how the children look at you. And then you too can just look at them, with results.

Of Diet and Defiance

Dear Dr. Ray,

Please comment on what seems an increasing societal trend: structuring a child's diet to reduce the frequency of active, impulsive, or defiant behavior.

Hungry for Answers

We are a microwave culture. We want results, effortlessly and certainly, in the shortest amount of time. Like everyone, I too am caught up in the quickening pace. In the morning, I put my mug into the microwave, push "sixty seconds," and then stand there practically pounding on the glass, "Come on! Let's go. I haven't got all minute."

What better, quicker, relatively effortless way to alter that often most puzzling and relentless of human phenomena—kids' behavior—than simply to make some savvy dietary adjustments or eliminations? In fact, listening to the expanding buffet of popular claims out there, we could easily get the impression that smoothing out Eaton's social and emotional development is only a few foodstuffs away.

Cut out the artificial, the red, the sweet, whatever remotely tastes good. Give Graham a dry cracked wheat tofu sandwich with bean sprouts, and he'll get better math scores and kiss his sister before he cleans her room.

The idea that smart, individually tailored eating plans can alter behavior for some kids, particularly the harder to handle ones, is enormously appealing. Indeed, our culture has swallowed the notion. "He went to a party last night. He had three peanut butter cups, two cans of cola, and a choco-surge. He came home and punched the dog. It had to be the choco-surge."

Give Graham a dry cracked wheat tofu sandwich with bean sprouts, and he'll get better math scores and kiss his sister before he cleans her room.

Probably not. The flaw with the belief that diet deters discipline is a major one: Research doesn't support it, at least nowhere near popular perception. Further, the one bad guy in the diet who does little damage, while most people think it does lots, is sugar. Repeated studies have shown that the great majority of kids are not behaviorally affected by sweet stuff. It does not make them more active, agitated, or "cranked."

At this point, let me say what I am not saying. I am not saying diet is unimportant. Obviously, it's critical to good health and fitness. I'm not saying that some children are not allergic physically to certain foods or ingredients, which can upset their whole system. And I'm not saying sugar is good for kids. What I *am* saying is that for most children, what they eat does not influence their actions anywhere near as much as is commonly thought.

What's more, the "bad foods make bad kids" notion is bad for parents. It can easily misdirect them away from the truly most powerful influence on their kids' behavior—themselves. It's just a whole lot easier to cut out a donut than to rethink and redo one's parenting. The former takes twenty seconds; the latter takes twenty years.

At this point, I can almost hear the e-mail dropping in the virtual basket as parents assert that they watch firsthand as their children change only mere minutes after ingesting a taboo food. I don't doubt that's what parents observe. The question is, What actually causes the change?

Besides the fact that our systems don't work that fast, there may be other, better explanations: the power of belief, the power of suggestion, the power of expectations, the association of naturally cranking events with goodies (for example, birthday parties, friends' visits, occasions of all kinds). In our society, food equals fun.

My comments on all this, I must confess, may not be totally objective. I have a deep personal interest in a weak sugar effect. Do you know how much candy, suckers, gum, and treats can come into a house when you take ten children trick-or-treating for two hours? If I were afraid of sugar, I'd be living in the shed now.

SEVEN

Misbehavior in Word

From the moment children enter our lives, we use language to raise them. Within a year or two they are using language to raise us. Even a little preschooler is a sophisticated verbal creature. Thus kids learn very early how to use words to get their way. As language is part of our human condition, so too using language to misbehave is part of our human condition.

There is no limit to how kids, using only words, can resist even the best parenting. There is a limit, however, to the kinds of verbal misconduct common to most kids. To be sure, actions often accompany a child's words, particularly when words alone don't work. For now, our focus will be on those trouble spots that are primarily wordy in nature. They are somewhat ordered by age, but almost any form of misconduct can cut a wide swath across many years.

One suggestion: Even if a question doesn't presently address your youngster's age or style, consider reading it anyway. The answer, while aimed at a particular problem, may have broader disciplinary usefulness.

Words Without End

Dear Dr. Ray,

How can I keep my kids from nagging? They hammer away at me until I either cave in or lose my temper. And the more tired I get, the harder they push.

Nagging Fears

Nagging illustrates a great paradox of parenthood. The more parents nag, the less kids respond. The more kids nag, the more parents respond. Are they smarter than we are? Do they have more psychological stamina?

Whatever the case, the reality is this: If nagging didn't work, kids wouldn't do it. Kids realize this after a few years of life. Parents realize it after a few kids.

Nagging illustrates a great paradox of parenthood. The more parents nag, the less kids respond. The more kids nag, the more parents respond.

The art of nagging is elegantly simple: Use relentless words in pursuit of a goal. The short-term goal is to get what you want. The long-term goal is to soften Mom or Dad's resistance to future nagging.

Compared to parents, children are relatively powerless. They don't have control over their environments as we do. So, through words—millions of them—comes their power to persuade. Kids count on our ears' tiring long before their vocal cords do.

Kids are typically more persistent than normal on two occasions. (Normal persistence is considered five to ten nags per minute.) The first is when they *really, really* want something, as opposed to the much less urgent, *really* want something.

Let's say you are considering granting Desiree a special treat or privilege. She can't chance that you'll make a decision based solely upon its merits, so she dramatically kicks up her level of pleading, begging, and overall obnoxiousness. A good way to short-circuit this verbal jack hammering is to say, "Don't ask again, even once, or the answer will be no. I need quiet to think."

Another prime nag-time is in public. Kids can smell it when you're parenting in fear of making a scene or of looking incompetent. That's their "go" signal. It doesn't take many nags to crack you in front of others, especially as the nags rise in volume.

How to escape this? "For every time you ask me, you'll sit five minutes at home." Or "Ask me once more, Avis, and we'll have to leave." Or "Nag, and next time I won't take you with me."

To break nagging's grip, you must not let it work. That's easy for me to write. I'm in my office listening to a radio I can unplug if I want. Kids don't have "off" buttons, but once they realize you will not be verbally browbeaten, they will look for other ways to get what they want. That's good, I think.

If you feel you can reach deep within and tap an unused reservoir of resolve, you could practice ignoring all nagging words. After you've said no to "Mom, can I ride the triple-spiral demon a seventeenth time?" act as though Constance is no longer speaking. In time—anywhere between a minute and a decade—she will wind down.

If you're like most of us parents and doubt your ability to stay oblivious for thousands of words at a time, or if you simply don't want to hear it, you could implement a gag order: "Tucker, if you nag, you will nag in your room." Or "You will write fifty times, 'Nagging is not a good way to communicate.'"

DISCIPLINE THAT LASTS A LIFETIME

Would fifty times constitute written nagging?

One mother simply asked, "Are you nagging?" She really was saying, "Don't nag, or there will be consequences." The kids knew the consequences. They had earned them a few dozen times before. So "Are you nagging?" was sufficient to silence them.

Days of Whine and Roses

Dear Dr. Ray,

My kids, ages five and nine, both whine constantly. Any ideas for getting them to speak in a normal tone?

Whine-Filled

Whining—words sort of sung in an off-key, E-flat tone. It's musical nagging. To say that whining gets on parents' nerves is like saying that acid rock music is mildly irritating when heard from a dentist's chair. Whine-weary parents have compared whining to the sound of fingernails scraping a blackboard, a buzz saw hitting a rusty nail, or a serrated file being dragged across the strings of a violin.

All kids whine to some degree. It's a weakness of their childish nature. But contrary to popular belief, not all kids outgrow the practice. Some grown-ups can still whine with the best of kids.

Prime whine time lies in the heart of childhood, roughly between ages three and ten. Adolescents would whine more if they didn't spend so much time being mad at us. Antagonism and whining are offsetting emotions.

Much whining is transitory. It comes and goes with the coming and going of a child's wants. As long as little Patience doesn't desire anything from you, she's less likely to whine. I mean, how often does she badger you with, "Awwww, Mom, I'd be sooooo happy if I could pull weeds all day."

Several approaches can help you tone down the frequency of your daughter's whining. The most basic is "planned stupor." Once the whining starts, you cease to respond. Act as though no one is even there.

As long as the whining wears on, you are oblivious. In time—anywhere between three minutes and twelve years—the pestering will die down. Honest. Kids get tired of talking to walls even quicker than parents do.

Of course, planned stupor requires tremendous stamina. Many, if not most, parents will admit they're not sure whether they can, or even want to, stand up to such relentless badgering until it tapers. Put another way, you might be able to endure the scraping of one fingernail on a blackboard for three seconds, but not thirty-four thousand nails dragging across it for nine hours.

If planned stupor is not appealing, you can turn to whine tactic #2: "deliberate distance." Wherever and whenever possible, as soon as the whining begins, put distance between your ears and Melody's vocal cords. You could leave the room, the house, maybe the country, but typically none of these is convenient or wise.

After all, why should you have to go anywhere? You're not the whiner. You're the whin-ee. So instead of your leaving, put Melody somewhere where you can't hear her voice, or where it's dampened enough to be bearable. Her room is one obvious place. Another is a "quiet chair," as psychologists call it. (Now there's a misnomer.)

You could even send her outside or downstairs. Do you have a whine cellar? Since her constant whining is infringing upon your rights, such as the right to be sane, you are well within your rights to deny her temporarily the privilege of being near you, or at least the privilege of whining near you.

A third option is the "anything whined for is not given" rule. If Melody whines for something, tell her once, "That's whining," and then don't give her what she's asking for. She has to ask appropriately to receive, the first time around.

Finally, to remind you and your youngsters that whining is not a form of communication that gets any results in your house, put a sign on your refrigerator door clearly spelling out "NO WHINE." You are making a promise: You will spell no whine before its time.

> You could even send her outside or downstairs. Do you have a whine cellar?

I'm Ba-ack

Dear Dr. Ray,

I can hardly visit with friends anymore because my children (ages five and three) interrupt us constantly. I send them to play but they keep returning.

Conversationless

You have several options.

One, quit visiting with friends. Tell them you have children now, and you won't be able to talk to any adults until your kids are teenagers and don't want to be around you anymore because you embarrass them.

Two, tell your friends to stop interrupting you and your children. You'll talk to them if and when your kids have to go to the bathroom. But warn them to speak quickly.

Three, teach your children to respect your visits with your friends by setting up some expectations for their behavior.

Obviously you haven't chosen options one and two because you still have friends left. I suspect you've tinkered with option three, but have been frustrated by your kids' crashing repeatedly through your expectations. I'm with you. I like option three best, too. Shortly we'll explore it.

> **By allowing Oral to be heard whenever he wants, we teach him not to respect other people's rights: not only the right to be heard, too, but also the right to hear people other than kids.**

There are at least three good reasons for permanently interrupting your children's interrupting. First, even good friends can take only so many exasperating visits. Parents of intrusive children often find their circle of conversational friends shrinking.

Second, though our culture has pretty much thrown off past generations' attitude of "children should be seen and not heard," the pendulum seems to have swung too far in the other direction. By allowing Oral to be heard whenever he wants, we teach him not to respect other people's rights: not only the right to be heard, too, but also the right to hear people other than kids.

Third, children are more likable, to us and to others, when

we don't allow them to be obnoxious. I mean, when was the last time you heard, "You know, I just love the way your children feel so free and comfortable barging into our conversation any time they want"?

One reason children are more pushy than they used to be is that many experts have convinced parents to allow them to be. They need to have loads of attention, so goes the reasoning, to form a healthy self-image. Therefore, when little Patience wants to talk, seeks your attention or approval, or just wants to show you something, you'd better drop what you're doing lest she feel neglected or unimportant.

In fact, children will not suffer a stunted self-image simply because they don't get every adult in their vicinity to suspend all conversations with others to meet their wants, however urgent they think those wants are. On the contrary, respect for grown-ups' relationships with others is a critical aspect of character. It helps kids accept that the universe does not rotate around them.

So how do you teach this respect? As you've probably already noticed, it's not enough simply to tell your kids, "We're visiting now. Go play." Or "Please don't interrupt. Say 'excuse me.'" The kids will comply, for a few tenths of a second, but they'll be back, in full verbal force.

You'll need to add some oomph to your requests. "Fulbright, please go play. The next time you come back and interrupt, you'll sit on the couch." In other words, put some consequences behind your expectations. You may have to repeat trips to the couch—or wherever—several times the next few visits, but the kids will catch on. When Mom says,

"Don't be rude," she means it.

I wanted to say a few more things, but my kids are bugging me. I wish they'd let me write. Every time I sit down with a pencil, they start. I've told them a million times, "Daddy has to work," but I just can't get them to ...

The Juvenile Inquisition

Dear Dr. Ray,

My son (age four) is very inquisitive. He's constantly asking me questions, and no matter how hard I try, I eventually get tired of answering and lose patience. It makes me feel guilty.

Asked Out

From the day my son could string together a noun and verb to form a semicoherent sentence, up to the age of five, I would guess he's asked me about five million questions. These range from the mundane ("Dad, how did you know that driver's name was 'Idiot'? Is he your friend?") to the physical ("Why don't stars fall down?") to the metaphysical ("Which is better, love or the angels?"). My favorite comes from circa age four: "How do we know I'm *really* Andrew?"

About a third of these I attempt to answer—generally the straightforward ones, such as how I knew Mr. Idiot. About a third I fudge: The sky is blue because it reflects the ocean—though it's usually only a matter of months before he challenges me on these. And in response to about a third I say, "Go ask your mother. She knows everything."

During a recent one-hour car trip with just my son, I decided

139

to count how many questions he would ask if I responded to the best of my knowledge. Having just watched six weeks of *Teen Jeopardy,* I was feeling pretty cocky.

His total? One hundred and thirty-seven. And this interrogation was interrupted halfway by a several-minute, twenty-eight-verse stint of "This Old Man." Honest. I counted again. It's my shrink nature. Now that I think back, the chorus started shortly after Andrew asked me whether I had ever seen a live dinosaur.

Relentless questions are children's early grappling with who they are, what the world is, how it works, and why it all is. By nature, some kids give voice to their wonder more than others, but almost all do, for years, until childlike curiosity fades, the television envelops them, or they become adolescents, who don't ask us anything because we have long ceased to know anything.

Through the wonderment years, we strive to stimulate, to answer all we can, so as not to snuff out even a molecule ("Dad, what's a molecule?") of their God-given voraciousness for life. As happens so often in parenthood, conflict inevitably arises when our spirit meets our flesh. ("What do you mean, Dad? Is that a ghost with skin?") We want to feed them, but we grow exhausted far sooner than they do. Their energy—physical, emotional, intellectual—dwarfs ours.

So try as we might to fudge, finagle, or find out the real answer to "Where do all the worms come from when it rains?" we can't keep up the pace. Sometimes we crack, exploding with some version of "Who are you, Einstein? Two years ago, you couldn't even use a toilet."

To quench your son's intellectual thirst, while not going dry yourself, here are a few ideas, most of which I've been forced to find through hard experience. ("Dad, is experience harder than diamonds?")

You are not an inadequate, psychologically stunting parent if you don't answer everything, or if you don't want to answer everything. Like most childhood qualities, inquisitiveness, however awesome in the raw, needs to be moderated some, or else it evolves to obnoxiousness. ("Dad, why did you ask Mom for a muzzle?")

Every parent varies in toler-

> So try as we might to fudge, finagle, or find out the real answer to "Where do all the worms come from when it rains?" we can't keep up the pace. Sometimes we crack, exploding with some version of "Who are you, Einstein? Two years ago, you couldn't even use a toilet."

ance, depending upon person-ality, fatigue, other children, and the pressures of life. Don't feel guilty because you need to take breaks. Wise parents call time-out before they get mad or mean or act like idiots. ("Dad, can people who don't drive cars be idiots?")

Don't answer everything yourself. Use your young assistant. "What do you think, Able? Can you answer that question?" At the least, you'll buy extra time before the next question. If any siblings are listening in, ask for their input, projecting confidence they'll think up a good answer. ("Dad, why do you always want me to answer my own questions? How can I do that if I don't know?")

Suggest alternatives to questions. I've dubbed this my "This Old Man" tactic. "Constance, I'll answer only two more questions. Then you can sing (or count clouds, or talk to Echo, or see how long you can be quiet). ("Dad, how come you always ask me to see how long I can be quiet?")

Again, you will not stifle your children's inquisitiveness. It's far too durable to be squelched by an occasional stop signal from you. Answer most of the questions some of the time or some of the questions most of the time. You'll not only reinforce their curiosity, you'll have more energy to give decent answers, or more believable fakes. ("Dad, how come last time you said that the moon is the brightest thing at night, and this time you said it doesn't have its own light?")

There's a bright side to questions without end. For the moment, no matter how many or fast they come, they're usually benign. Twelve years from now, though far less in number, they'll hit harder. ("Dad, what would you say if I told you the principal is going to call you tonight?") I personally would rather field a thousand "Can a gorilla beat up a tiger?" questions than one of those adolescent gems.

Just one more thing: Is a preschooler harder to discipline than an adolescent? Then how come they call it the terrible twos? Does that mean there's twins? Do they need two mommies?

A Cure for Tattling: Hear No Evil

Dear Dr. Ray,

My son and daughter, ages eight and five, seem to be having a contest over who can tattle on the other more. I'm at the point where I don't want to hear another accusation of any kind. How can I end this constant tattling?

Tattle-Weary

Kids like to tattle. It seems to arise from some juvenile sense of justice. As little Benedict sees it, there's no way he can idly stand by as his sister gets away with the very same things he tries to get away with. That simply isn't fair, and it must be stopped.

Basic tattling comes in several forms. Most straightforward is the *do you know what he did?* tattle, designed simply to get a sibling into hot water. "Mom. Cliff just climbed on the couch again." Here the tattler benevolently leaves the form of discipline up to you, the parent. She just wants to make sure you're aware of the transgression.

Then there's the more urgent *do something about her* tattle. "Make Iris quit looking at me." In this instance the tattle-worthy offense, looking, is brought to your attention, along with the demand that you do your parenting duty, *now.*

Most hardcore is the *don't just look at him, do something* tattle. "I can't believe you're letting him talk to you like that. You never let *me* use that word, in that tone of voice yet!" Here the tattler makes sure not only to point out what you're already aware of, but also to pressure you into feeling that if you don't take action, you're being lazy, unfair, or—heaven forbid—inconsistent in your discipline.

Probably the simplest way to silence tattling is to ignore it. Set up a house rule: Tattled words are unheard words. If you didn't see what happened, or if you have no solid evidence of misconduct, you will not act.

Obviously, if you spy Rufus hanging upside down from the spouting or Harry shows you his bald spot where Cutler snipped a chunk of his hair while he was sleeping, you may want to investigate further. But on the whole, the stuff of day-to-day tattling is highly ignorable, however highly irritating. Then too, if you try to ferret out the degree of truth of every tattle, you risk opening a can of worms, filled with tattles and countertattles, but short on facts.

"Ripley, whenever you tattle on Angel, whatever happens to her will happen to you."

To quiet inveterate tattlers—those whose main aim seems to be to shadow their siblings and make their lives miserable by reporting to you in graphic detail every misstep—you might consider a more active approach. "Ripley, whenever you tattle on Angel, whatever happens to her will happen to you." For instance, if Angel has to sit inside for fifteen minutes because, according to Ripley, she flung the kickball over the house again after being tagged "out," Ripley too will cool down for fifteen minutes inside. Essentially, his tattling is being directly disciplined because its sole intent is to make life difficult for his sister, and not to guide you in her upbringing.

With either method, must you worry that you're teaching your kids never to monitor each other's behavior and never to act responsibly if the situation calls for it? Absolutely not. Tattling is a far cry from genuine sibling concern. Tattling is endlessly bringing to your attention minor scrapes and childish conduct that you'd be better off just overlooking. A chronic tattler knows, or will quickly learn, what you'll attend to and what you won't.

There's a bright side to tattling. It should leave no doubt in your mind that your kids know exactly what you expect. Even while Polly is tattling, she's also telling you loud and clear that she knows what is right and what is wrong, what is allowed and what isn't.

The Appeals Process

Dear Dr. Ray,

What can I do about kids who run back and forth between my husband and me until they wrangle out of one of us the answer they want?

Exhausted by Appeals

If we were to ask kids what they like about having Mom and Dad around, we'd likely hear, "Because if one says 'No,' we can ask the other." Psychologists have their ideas about the benefits of two parents living in the same household. But if we were to ask kids what they like about having Mom and Dad around, we'd likely hear, "Because if one says 'No,' we can ask the other."

It's called "appealing the decision." Most expert kids have mastered the appeals process, which includes only a few standard steps:

1. Make sure a room, wall (preferably brick), or miles are between Mom and Pop, thus making it inconvenient, or ideally, impossible for one to confirm whether the other really said, "OK, you can have the car all weekend if you dust the coffee table first."

2. Use perfect timing. Wendell will approach Mom with the appeal to go over to Perry's house and watch *The Video Game That Ate Chicago* only after Dad has left for the store, taking his negative answer with him. Or Dad is underneath a disassembled lawn tractor when the appeal comes: "Mom said she

thinks you should let me trim the bushes *after* I play basketball so my muscles will already be warmed up."

3. Use appeal jargon. "Mom said to ask you; Dad told me it's OK with him if it's OK with you; Mom said we could, but we wanted to tell you because you're our dad." Watch out for this last one. As you're swelling with pride, you may hear, "Dad, do you have an extra ten bucks you don't want?"

4. When all else fails, use guilt. "How come you never let us do anything that Mom says is OK? You always say no; it never does me any good to ask you anything." If you deny the appeal, prepare yourself to hear "guilty, as charged."

One way drastically to cut appeals is for you and your spouse to cease deferring decisions to each other. Decide yourself whether or not Holmes can stay up until midnight reading *Family Law in Action*. Don't put it in the hands of your spouse.

Because kids have the mental agility of trial lawyers, they won't always be quietly deterred by your no-appeals stance. Therefore, you may have to render a few other verdicts.

Verdict #1: Any decision made initially by one parent will automatically be upheld by the other, whether he or she agrees with it or not. No doubt you and your spouse will disagree at times, but iron out your differences later, out of court, away from Perry and Mason. The more often you and your spouse openly disagree, the more appeals you'll hear.

Verdict #2: Whenever Perry appeals a decision, ask him if he's already been given an answer. If yes, refer to Verdict #1. If he falsifies the record and tells you he received a yes when he really got a no, Perry will pay the consequences for his fraudulent actions. For example, if he claims that your spouse said he could go swimming now and sweep out the garage later, when in fact it was sweep then swim, he will have to weed the flower bed in addition to sweeping the garage when he returns, along with losing his swimming privileges for a week.

Why do kids continue to appeal decisions even after their parents have caught on? They're certainly not slow to learn our ways. Nor are they trying to be underhanded. No, their motivation is straightforward: They've got nothing to lose and much to gain.

At worst, they'll just hear again what they didn't want to hear the first time around. At best, they could get a verdict overturned or at least a hung jury. And this provides invaluable information for future requests. They know who is better to ask first.

Deft Denying Act

Dear Dr. Ray,

How can I get my ten-year-old son to admit when he's done something wrong? He's so convincing in his denial that I sometimes wonder if he can tell truth from fiction.

The Interrogator

Kids can bend, fold, and mutilate the truth with spectacular creativity. Ripley can weave unbelievable stories about how he single-handedly saved the whole third grade from a bull elephant rampaging through the cafeteria. Linus can convince you he truly is the only kid in the whole school whom the principal trusts to drive his mobile home to the prom.

Of all the ways that kids can warp reality, perhaps the most common, yet worrisome for parents, is the deft denying act, or "I'm innocent even if you prove me guilty." Here's a typical scenario.

You know—or have a "preponderance of evidence"—that Wiley spray-painted "I love Gypsy" on the front door. When confronted, without flinching he looks you right in the eye and asserts his innocence with such conviction that you consider hiring a handwriting analyst to check out his story. Indeed, you could show Wiley a videotape of him spraying his love note, letter by letter, only to hear him finally confess, "I'll admit from this angle it looks like me. But you see how you can't quite make out my face? That's a stunt kid."

What makes kids close their eyes to the facts staring them in the face? Contrary to parental worry, kids do recognize the truth. They know reality from unreality. They may deny knowing what they did was wrong, but they know what they did.

Furthermore, almost never in these instances do they suffer from some psychological block or selective amnesia. On the contrary, kids have incredible memories. How many other human beings do you know who could recall the exact day and hour six years ago when you did absolutely nothing to his brother for writing "I love Mommy" in crayon on the television? A youngster will remember what's in his best interests to remember and "forget" what's in his best interests to forget, like the fact that just twenty-seven seconds ago he turned the front door into a seven-foot Valentine's Day card.

What is the motive for such deft denying acts? It's usually quite straightforward: To escape the impending consequences of their actions.

If that means denying to the last breath that he was anywhere on the continent when the trouble occurred, Wiley will try it. He figures, "What do I have to lose?" Even if your voice is suspiciously calm, your clenched teeth and crossed eyes betray you're upset. Wiley knows you're on the edge of disciplinary action—he knows that's not *really* a stunt kid on the video—so he's struggling to kindle in your mind at least one flicker of doubt as to his culpability.

Maybe you'll finally drop the inquisition, and with it any discipline. And even if you don't, he can still salvage something by playing the unjustly accused martyr: "My dictator dad made me clean the front door that was spray-painted by some kids who love my girlfriend."

> Of all the ways that kids can warp reality, perhaps the most common, is the deft denying act, or "I'm innocent even if you prove me guilty."

When are you most likely to witness a deft denying act? One, when you "know" your son is guilty, but couldn't prove it in a court of law. For example, Wiley was the only one home for the past three hours, and when you left, the lamp was still in one piece on top of the TV.

Two, when Wiley's done something seemingly inexplicable or "out of character." Kids proclaim their innocence so often after stealing something that I've come to view the two behaviors as a package duo.

Three, when Wiley has acted impulsively. "I hit her because she sneezed during my favorite commercial." Even he is confused as to why he did it, so he denies doing it.

All things considered, occasional bouts of deft denying do not a liar make. In and of themselves they are not a sign of major psychological problems. However, lying still must be dealt with firmly, or it could become a style.

Generally, the more you claw and scrape for the truth, the deeper the hole Linus will dig trying to cover his tracks, and the more agitated you'll become.

On to the next question: How can you cancel a deft denying act? First, try to stay calm or at least try to *look* calm. For parents, a state of complete calm is generally not achieved until somewhere around four years after the last child leaves home. In the meantime, though, if you keep reminding yourself that Linus' denial is not a warning of future emotional maladjustment, but rather is a "right now" stab at escaping discipline, you won't feel quite so panicky.

Also, you won't feel quite so intense an urge to drag out the truth through six hours of nonstop interrogation under bright lights. Generally, the more you claw and scrape for the truth, the deeper the hole Linus will dig trying to cover his tracks, and the more agitated you'll become.

One of the more effective ways to bring forth the facts is the "Truth or Consequences" approach. Let's say that you have just returned home from running an errand. You were gone for seventeen minutes. During your absence, Truman found and devoured a two-pound bag of Oreo cookies.

Although you didn't actually catch him red-handed (or

should I say "fudge-handed"), you know Tru is your man. He was the only one home, and cookie-smudged fingerprints are all over the refrigerator and the VCR. Of course, Truman denies knowing there were even cookies in the house.

Don't argue. Don't confuse him with facts. Simply state: "Truman, I know what the truth is. So I will ask you only once about the cookies. If you own up to the truth, you'll have to pay me for the cookies. If you don't, you'll pay me for the cookies, *and* you'll have no cookies for the next week. So think about this carefully: Did you eat the Oreos?" Accept with a quiet nod whatever answer Truman gives you and *follow through* with your consequences.

About half the time parents first try "Truth or Consequences," they hear the truth. On the other hand, don't be surprised if after your calm minispeech, Truman mutters "What Oreos?" Remember, your main aim is to teach him that it's in his best interests to tell the truth. If he immediately acts in his best interests, he's learned fast. And if he doesn't, there's always next time. Your lesson will eventually soak in.

But what happens if you're not totally sure of the facts? Then you have to do what parents have to do dozens of times every day: Make a judgment call. If there's enough evidence to act, do so. You could be wrong, but in my opinion it's better to act in good faith according to the evidence than to wait until you are 100 percent sure of every move you make. Seldom do parents have the luxury of perfect certainty.

Boring Me to Tears

Dear Dr. Ray,

Will you please give me a response to my kids' constant "I'm bored"? How can they be?

Tired of Hearing It

What frustrates us "never have time to be bored" parent types is that our kids shouldn't be bored. They have, it seems, ten times the fun options we did as kids. Their world is more electronically dazzling, more toy-gorged, more minute-by-minute planned—all around, just more entertaining. How could they actually say, "There's nothing to do. I'm bored"?

What further chafes us is that we regularly do back flips to amuse Oscar, to give him neat new experiences. Which brings us to the rub. A basic law of human nature says: The more we are entertained, the quicker we become bored. So when kids complain of boredom, it's usually a sign that they've grown accustomed to being entertained, by you or by life, and not a sign that their existence is truly devoid of excitement.

> **A basic law of human nature says: The more we are entertained, the quicker we become bored.**

To assess whether this is the case for your kids, ask yourself some questions. How much TV do they watch? How many video games flash and beep at them? What's the level of their toy inventory? How much do you take responsibility for their amusement? How many scheduled activities pack their lives?

None of these things in and of themselves necessarily cause

problems. It's their cumulative effect, especially in high doses, that can teach a child that life is here to keep you interested, with little effort on your part.

"I'm bored" for many parents also rings of "I'm ungrateful." Instead of appreciating how much she does have, Jade is discontent when life isn't stimulating her to the degree she thinks it should.

So how can you teach Jade and Oscar that sometimes life is fun and sometimes it's dull—and when it's dull, you look to yourself to create enjoyment and not to others, especially Mom?

As with most aspects of child rearing, effective lessons are taught through action, not words. Whenever you see the entertainment mentality rearing its ugly head, cut the hours of television. Limit video games. Slash toy inventories. Reconsider some of the extracurriculars.

All this seems backward, doesn't it? How does reducing the fun options lead to less boredom? In the short run, it doesn't. The kids most likely will squawk and wail over their impoverished lifestyle. But in the long run, you will force them to become more self-directed. They will have to learn how to occupy their time. Then too, your time with them will be more enjoyable, as you move from "cruise activities" director back to mom, from party planner to parent.

Now onto the "I'm bored" words themselves. If you're bored of hearing them, here are several options.

1. Don't respond. Just return an amazed look that says, "How could you possibly be?" and walk away. In time—anywhere

between tomorrow and their wedding rehearsal dinner—your kids will realize that "I'm bored" doesn't prod mother into action.

2. "I'm bored" automatically leads to a) an essay on the pleasures of life, b) ten synonyms for "activity" (or similar words) from the dictionary, defined and used in sentences, c) a written list of ten, or twenty, or whatever number of "things I'm grateful for."

3. Create a "Bore Chores" jar. (This is my favorite.) Put a number of routine household chores on slips of paper into a jar or box. Tell the kids that whenever you hear that somebody's bored, you will assume they are asking for something to do. Whereupon they will be referred to, as one adolescent put it, the jar of torture. And don't just threaten it. Expressed boredom leads to chores, period.

The above suggestions should pretty quickly decrease the verbal complaints. They won't eliminate the attitude. That will take a while.

At times your kids may mope around with long faces that say, "I'm still bored but I can't even express my feelings because you're so stifling." Weather it. That should pass, too.

If it doesn't, you can always exercise your God-given parental prerogative to read faces: "You know, you look like you need something to do. I have plenty for you." Whereupon you'll probably hear some variant of "Oh, no, Mom, I was just deeply lost in thought about what I want to do next because I have so much to choose from. I'm really not bored at all." It's a miracle.

Cutting Back Back Talk

Dear Dr. Ray,

My five children are ages fifteen, fourteen, eleven, nine, and six. Their personalities are all very different. One thing they all do, though, is talk back. It's the source of most of our arguments.

Never the Last Word

Back talk—the universal misbehavior. Where children are, it is. Unless, of course, the children absolutely never need limits or discipline, you know, unreasonable things such as going to bed before the birds wake up, eating supper with the family, and putting their shoes away before the smoke alarm goes off.

Since your youngsters fall into two age groups—the preteen and the teen—let's talk back talk in two categories: first for younger kids, then for older kids (and maybe spouses, too).

Basic back talk comes in two types: grumble talk and nasty talk. Grumble talk is clearly the more benign. It is essentially Polly's editorial comment about the way you're raising her or running the house: "I'm just a worker around here. How'd you keep the house clean before I was born?" "This is the fourth time this week I've had to hang up my coat." "You never let me look at you like that when I was two. How come he gets away with it?"

Grumble talk isn't usually disrespectful. It's more of a whiney, maybe feebly, provocative attempt to pull you into an argument. Since it takes two to tangle, if you ignore it, most grumble talk will die out from lack of fuel. Quietly shrug off Polly's complaining, so long as she is hanging up her coat for the fourth time this week or is doing the cruel work you ask of her.

Fill the dog's water bowl again? How can you drive her so hard? Sometimes, what can you really say? Maybe she *is* the only ninth-grader in school who has to do her homework before she does her nails.

One good way to discriminate between nasty talk and grumble talk is to ask yourself: How would I react to this if it came from another adult?

Grumble talk doesn't typically escalate into verbal warfare if you can develop an attitude of "You can express your opinion, as long as it's not disrespectful or nasty, and as long as you meet your responsibility." In other words, if Polly is doing what you ask, you can't always expect her to be happy about it.

Whereas grumble talk generally can be soothed with little response, nasty talk, on the other hand, requires action. Nasty talk is abusive, disrespectful, or directly challenging to your rights and authority: "Don't tell me what to do." "You're stupid if you think I'm going to do that." "Get off my back." "I don't have to listen to you—just shut up."

One good way to discriminate between nasty talk and grumble talk is to ask yourself: How would I react to this if it came from another adult? Nasty talk is talk that doesn't keep people friends very long.

Nasty talk is not expressing feelings. It is verbal meanness. And the younger children are when they learn to control it, the better for them and for others. All kids misbehave. But nasty talk, if left uncurbed, feeds on itself and can become a chronic challenge to your right to discipline in your child's best interests.

Consequences for nasty talk need to be firm and certain. Here are four suggestions for kids between ages three and twelve.

1. Each bout of nastiness leads to standing in a corner, sitting at the table with head down, or heading for their room anywhere from five minutes to a half hour or more, depending upon a child's age. Time doesn't begin until all is quiet, and time starts over if trouble starts over.

When choosing a corner, you might want it to be in a room other than the one you're in. You won't be so likely to hear: "Am I done yet?" "I promise I'll be good forever." "I have to potty." "I wish Daddy were my mommy." "I hate this house, and the garage, too."

2. For nasty talk, Gabby will a) write twenty-five times (or some chosen amount) a sentence of your choosing; or b) copy a hundred-word-or-more paragraph, which you've composed, on self-control, respect for others, controlling anger, and so on; or c) compose her own paragraph, with the length depending upon the severity of the outburst. My father claims he should have assigned me a few one-million-word essays when I was a kid.

157

3. Disrespect leads to work. For instance, John Henry owes you fifteen minutes' worth of chores, or a job from your "job jar," especially compiled for such occasions. Maybe he needs to burn off some energy.

4. If you want to teach respect all around, how about holding yourself answerable to the same standards? We grown-ups really have no more right to talk mean to the kids than they do us. We have the right to discipline, but not to be nasty about it.

How about a 150-word written apology to your son for verbally blistering him last night? Do this a few times, and if nothing else, your kids will think you've slipped over the edge. Maybe they'll feel sorry for you, and out of mercy talk back less.

Which consequences you use depend upon your child's age and your preference. The content of your sentences or whether you choose a dining room chair over a corner is not nearly as important as your predictability. Your consequences are automatic.

Finally, remember: What constitutes nasty talk is your judgment, not Gabby's. Debate it with her, and she'll give you that dumbfounded look that says, "What? I didn't say anything. What tone of voice? My lips never moved."

Now on to reducing back talk from adolescents. The ideas are similar, with a little fine tuning.

Even the sweetest, non-lippy child can become lippy as he matures—or immatures—into adolescence. As kids get older, they increasingly believe their way, not yours, is the way to see things. In and of itself, that is not unhealthy. In fact, it's part of growing up. Conflicts can arise, however, when Gabby constantly questions your decisions, in terms that can't be considered diplomatic, to say the least.

The amount of back talk seems to peak somewhere between a child's thirteenth and fifteenth years. It usually holds steady for a few years after that, and then starts to decline.

Even the sweetest, non-lippy child can become lippy as he matures—or immatures—into adolescence. As kids get older, they increasingly believe their way, not yours, is the way to see things.

As with preteens, a high percentage of adolescent back talk is grumble talk. They're intent on complaining. They may be upset, but they're not getting nasty or defiant: "Dry the dishes already? They're still wet!" or "If I turn the stereo down any further, I might as well turn it off."

Sometimes you can defuse grumble talk by agreeing with it. For example:

"This is the third time I've taken out the garbage this week!"

"That's true."

Or "I always have to make my bed."

"Yes, you do."

You're not being sarcastic. You're matter-of-factly acknowledging that what your youngster is grumbling about is the way it is. With you agreeing, there's nobody left for Storm to grumble against.

Teens are also masters of the mumble grumble. The technique is straightforward. Turn your back on the closest adult and walk away muttering discontentedly under your breath, just loud enough to let her know something is being said, but just soft enough so she can't make it out.

Your instinctive response to mumble grumble might be to demand, "What did you say?" More than likely, you'll receive the likes of "I didn't say anything. Can't a guy even talk to himself around here?" Yet you know he's talking to you; he never talks to himself in that tone of voice.

Here you have two choices. One, you can pretend you didn't at all hear what you can't quite hear, using the "prodigal son" principle: If he's doing what you've asked, he's allowed to be unhappy about it. Or two, you can place a price on mumble grumble. Some prices are listed below under ways to deal with nasty talk.

As we noted before, nasty talk is distinctly different from grumble talk. It is defiant, disrespectful, or challenging in tone or content. It carries a hostile "Don't tell me what to do" message. Like grumbling, the level of nasty talk typically also rises with the advent of teenhood.

Nasty talk is talk that needs consequences placed upon it. Otherwise, it can escalate in frequency and ugliness. Here are ideas for consequences. Very important point: These must be linked to each instance of nasty talk.

- Compose an essay on self-control, respect for others, or expressing feelings appropriately. The topic and length are your choice. Review the essay with your child, discussing its ideas and complimenting his or her thoughtfulness.

- Look up, define, and use in a sentence ten dictionary words (three syllables or more, not "a, an, the"). Keep a dictionary handy, say, near the kitchen table. If you have a particularly tough-talking teen, you may need a dictionary in every room.

This approach was one mother's favorite. Her attitude was "If you have to talk like that, you need a better vocabulary." By the time her son was fourteen, he had the highest vocabulary test scores in his high school.

- Use the dictionary creatively. Find and define ten words with a "z" in the middle. Or define fifteen words ending in "ion." When my dad was really upset, he'd threaten me with "You can't leave the kitchen table until you find ten words that begin with 'qx.'"

- Levy a monetary fine upon nasty talk. Teenagers may like to talk poorly, but they don't like to be poor.

- The reverse of nasty talk is respect. What privileges can your teen earn by exercising self-control for, say, two days? Gradually lengthen the time required to earn perks, such as extended curfew or phone times. Ask your teen what he or she would like to earn, within reason. (Otherwise, you could hear, "An unchaperoned trip to Daytona Beach.")

Grumble talk and nasty talk are normal teenage phenomena. They'll disappear with maturity as long as you teach your teen that neither mode of communication is an acceptable way to converse in your home.

With Respect to Feelings

Dear Dr. Ray,

I encourage my children (ages ten, twelve, and fifteen) to express themselves, but sometimes they get pretty hostile. I want open communication, but I don't want back talk. Is there one without the other?

Listening Too Much?

If you can't have one without the other, tact and diplomacy are headed the way of chivalry. Encouraging some freedom of expression promotes two-way respect. A youngster will feel he has received a fair hearing, and a parent will feel more fair for having allowed it.

Nevertheless, allowing unrestrained freedom of expression promotes two-way disrespect. Young Burne may be the one who heats up the exchange, but soon we're matching hot word for hot word. Despite our best intentions, we can't quietly withstand open assault for long. Our desire for free communication will be overcome by our instinct for self-respect. Communication without rules doesn't foster feelings; it hurts them.

Put another way, open communication does not mean license to speak one's mind in whatever tone at whatever volume with whatever words. Full freedom of opinion is benevolent parenthood. Full freedom of expression is not.

As your children move deeper into adolescence and become more deeply opinionated, particularly about your conduct, you might want to establish some freedom of speech guidelines, in order to promote the common good and to semi-insure domestic tranquillity:

1. You can all say your piece as long as it's said peacefully.

2. The speaker has the right to remain uninterrupted as long as he or she remains respectful.

3. As soon as communication turns ugly, the right to be heard is temporarily forfeited.

A major clarification is in order here. What constitutes disrespect is a parent's judgment. Kids have a far more tolerant definition of disrespect than we do. They don't consider themselves nasty until they're tipping tables and tossing bricks. And then it still depends on whether they hit anything.

Kids don't consider themselves nasty until they're tipping tables and tossing bricks. And then it still depends on whether they hit anything.

Probably the simplest way to deal with unfeeling expression is to call a halt to it. In Congress, this is called invoking cloture. (I think it comes from the Old English phrase "Cloture mouth!") A brief, firmly enforced separation—in a room, chair, whatever—apart from you should restore calm. If it doesn't, you probably will have to respond as we talked about previously in dealing with back talk: levy a penalty, such as a two-hundred-word essay on respect, a report from the encyclopedia, a fifty-cent fine, an extra chore, or an hour-earlier bedtime.

After your patient explaining of the guidelines, after your admirable refusal to respond in kind—or unkind—to disrespect, don't be too surprised if your children still think you're stifling their First Amendment rights. Just because a rule is fair and ultimately makes for more freedom doesn't mean kids will like it. It takes time to understand the benefit of such unnatural things as restraint and tact.

There is a bright side to all of this. At least the kids can take advantage of your new set of guidelines to tell you what they think of your new set of guidelines. If they do it respectfully, of course.

EIGHT

Misbehavior in Deed

"Sticks and stones may break my bones, but words can never hurt me." Not true. A child's words alone can challenge, frustrate, and hurt parents. Couple those words with actions, and now you've got a one-two punch that can temporarily knock the best of parents off their feet.

Fortunately, as with word misconduct, most action misconduct is pretty basic stuff. The typical kid is more relentless than creative. In a way that's good. It dramatically narrows the range of trouble parents have to be prepared for.

As before, the following questions are ordered generally from younger to older ages, but there are really no clear boundary lines from age to age and misbehavior to misbehavior. While some scenarios are more common to certain ages, any kid worthy of the name can jump years ahead to try new stuff or to revisit old patterns. To be fully prepared, you just might have to read everything.

Too Pooped to Pop

Dear Dr. Ray,

I have one child, a three-year-old daughter. She'd been completely toilet trained for a year. The past several weeks she's slipped back into messing her pants. I'm not sure what's going on.

What Now?

First consult your physician to rule out any physical cause for your daughter's toilet training trouble. Once given the physical all clear, you can approach this behavior from a psychological angle. Fancy terms for bowel training problems are "encopresis" and "fecal soiling." For our purposes, we will use the shirtsleeve, or maybe I should say "pant leg," term "soiling."

Since your daughter is your only child you can also rule out one of the more common causes of resoiling: adjustment to a new sibling. The arrival of a baby brother or sister temporarily leads some kids to behave a bit babyish themselves. And what more natural way to act babyish than to forsake the "grown-up" potty in favor of one's pants.

Often you can't figure out where the soiling is coming from—psychologically speaking, that is. Nevertheless, you still have to handle it, again psychologically speaking.

Sometimes change or stress in a child's life will lead to a toileting backslide: the start of preschool, a new sitter, Mom returning to work, a family conflict. In these cases, once the underlying cause changes or is accepted by the child, the soiling often ceases. In fact, more often than not, kids have to accept change because it's reality: That new little one is here to stay. And you're not about to ask your new boss to give you three months off to retoilet train your preschooler.

Often you can't figure out where the soiling is coming from—psychologically speaking, that is. Nevertheless, you still have to handle it, again psychologically speaking. A first step is to try to stay calm.

This is a tall order, because toilet training is where the earliest power struggles can erupt. If Petunia catches wind that she can fire you up just by performing an act of nature, she may not resist the urge. If you must wail and gnash your teeth, then leave the room or hide behind the furnace. But don't let Petunia know she's got the upper hand (or lower body).

The next step is emotionally easier but takes more stamina. Whenever any of your senses tells you that Petunia has soiled (without your permission, that is), require that she immediately clean all dirtied clothes by rinsing them in the sink or tub—not for two swishes as she wishes, but for several minutes, long enough to make any fun become drudgery, as laundry should be. Your purpose is not to clean the clothes, but to hold Petunia accountable for her mess. Most likely you'll have to stand over each washing—without talking—but in the long run you'll save both you and Petunia a lot of wasted energy.

The hand laundry approach may take about a month or so to clear up the problem completely. If you want something faster, here's another strategy, but it takes even more stick-to-it-iveness on your part.

Every time Petunia soils, immediately place her on the potty for five minutes, telling her this is to allow her to complete any unfinished business. Thereafter, every two hours—no matter what Petunia is doing, except sleeping—place her back on the potty for five minutes. Let her know she can leave the potty before five minutes ends if she uses it. Otherwise, she must sit until the timer sounds.

These timely potty sittings occur for one twenty-four-hour cycle of complete control. In other words, if Petunia doesn't soil for one full day, the potty visits are over, *until* she again soils, at which time her sittings begin again and continue until twenty-four clean hours have passed. This method works especially well for older children who had been trained for some time and then backslid. Whichever approach you choose, the common thread is calmness and stamina.

Please write me again in a few months and let me know how things came out.

Tantrums: Normal Abnormal

Dear Dr. Ray,

My son is four years old. He's very lovable, but he has a temper that is explosive. I think his anger goes beyond normal bounds. He throws at least one tantrum a day. We're looking for ideas.

Shell-Shocked

Peak temper tantrum years are commonly understood to lie between ages two and six. By that standard, your son is smack in his prime. Actually, temper tantrums can erupt at any time in childhood—for that matter, at any time in adulthood. The underlying emotions, frustration and anger, are the same across all ages.

The tantrum itself is what changes. A fifteen-year-old may not fling herself to the floor, flail all body parts in opposing directions, choke back her breath, and wildly punch the air or herself. (I said, *may* not.) But as any parent of an adolescent can witness firsthand, older kids are quite capable of their own brand of temper display.

Your worry that your son's anger isn't normal is understandable, especially if you have to mimic a tornado drill during his tirades. Rest assured, your son is not abnormal.

First, he averages only a few blowups per day. Regularly I see children who throw fits almost as naturally as they breathe, and they suffer from nothing psychologically out of whack. They just let their anger loose too often and too spectacularly, and they need to be taught some self-control.

Second, by their nature, temper tantrums can appear bizarre, even scary. Storm's spine is twisting into the letter "Q." Her eyes are darting independently toward her ears. Sounds never before recorded in nature are bursting from her mouth.

Standard parental reaction to this level of emotional convulsion is something like "I know kids get mad, but this is not normal." Yes, it is.

Sparky is upset, or frustrated, or disappointed at you, Mom, because you're not letting him do what he'd like, or at the world because it's not spinning quite as he thinks it should, so he's letting every emotion hang out. Why? Because he hasn't yet grown into better self-control or incorporated the world's rules about such things as self-restraint and verbal tact.

In short, temper is when little children get overwhelmed by some big emotions. They don't know what to do with them, so they react loud and hard.

Of course, there's a bright side to temper tempests. On a miniature scale, they're reminders of what we can look like when we lose control. Not a pretty sight, is it?

At the same time, never have I seen a child emotionally scarred from a prolonged temper outburst. Anger itself causes no psychological damage, nor does it automatically indicate any. On the other hand, I have seen many children whose temper has become more regular and intense because it succeeded in manipulating shell-shocked adults to yield to childish demands.

Certainly expressing anger or feelings is not unhealthy. How it's expressed is what needs to be dealt with. Children need to learn to express emotions constructively and with some diplomacy. Screeching like an air-raid siren, spitting, biting chairs, and swinging at anything within arm's reach are not choice ways for anyone, even little kids, to win friends and influence people. The younger children are when they are taught this, the easier the teaching will be on them and their parents, not to mention the rest of the world.

> Screeching like an air-raid siren, spitting, biting chairs, and swinging at anything within arm's reach are not choice ways for anyone, even little kids, to win friends and influence people.

Do any kids exist who don't even occasionally pitch fits? Yes, I saw one once on TV who didn't. But most real world kids do.

Life is marked by disappointments and frustrations, even for a four-year-old. Just because tantrums are a phenomenon of nature, though, does not at all mean you should tolerate them.

Temper displays take two forms—the theatrical and the destructive. On their face, theatrical tantrums look spectacular, even violent. On closer notice, no one or nothing is really being attacked or damaged.

There are no teeth marks in the kitchen table. The cat's tail is still attached. The carpet is getting a full-body massage, but its fibers are not being ripped out one by one. Almost all that's being assaulted is the air, and it can take a beating and bounce right back. Noise volume may approach pain threshold, but overall, theatrical temper tantrums (TTT) are all show.

The quickest way to cancel a TTT is to give Barrymore what he's ranting for. Let him repeatedly take the phone off the hook because he likes to hear the recording "Please hang up and try your call again." He'll calm fast, but he'll learn to throw another, probably louder and longer, fit next time he wants to mis-play with something else (like the microwave, so he can dry his steel truck).

In the long run a good way to end theatrical performances is to exit stage right. In parent language, leave the scene. As long as you, the audience, is watching, the production has a purpose. Talulah is hoping you'll eventually yield to her wants, out of fear or exhaustion, or in search of every parent's primal desire—peace.

If it's impossible physically to move from "ground zero" (technical language for the center of a highly powerful blast), you have other options. One, turn your back until the show is over. Two, get ear plugs or cotton—for *your* ears, not Barrymore's. Let him hear himself; he might scare himself into silence. Three, stare into space with the most vacant look you can muster. Your goal is to convey oblivion.

To fight drama with drama, one mother told me she would drop to the floor at first sound of a tantrum and mimic her son's every move, I guess until he gave up or gave her what she wanted (silence) just to shut her up. Another parent would quietly hold a mirror in front of his daughter until she ceased her display, probably through being distracted by the maniac in the mirror.

Any of these styles can work. The common threads through all of them are these: first, the tantrum doesn't succeed in causing the folks to buckle under, and second, nobody except the child is getting visibly upset over the current situation. I suppose one could argue that the mimicking mom looks upset. But she really isn't. And her son knows that.

Destructive tantrums (DT's) are a force of a different color. They hurt people or damage things—defenseless chairs, innocent walls, or pathetic, always walked-upon carpets. Destructive tantrums must be actively and firmly stopped. Ignoring them isn't usually practical, because something is being assaulted, whether you are paying attention or not.

Here again, you can choose from an assortment of strategies. You might physically restrain Gale until he quiets, and then place him someplace to sit for a while. You might swat his seat (his behind, not the chair). This may not totally stop him, but it could throw him into a more benign TTT. You might send, or possibly take, him to his room to simmer down. He can rejoin civilization when you think it wise.

Sometimes destructive fits leave damage in their wake before you can intercept them. Here, as young as Rocky is, he should still clean his shoe marks off the wall, or pay to fix the chair through money he earns from small household chores that you set up. The guiding rule for a damaging temper eruption is this: As much as possible for a four-year-old, Rocky makes right what he did wrong.

DISCIPLINE THAT LASTS A LIFETIME

There's a bright side to temper tempests. After an explosive performance, Conan has expended so much energy that he's too tired to misbehave for a while. At least for the next three or four minutes, until he gets his second wind.

Lost During the Storm

Dear Dr. Ray,

When my six-year-old son loses his temper, it doesn't matter what discipline I impose, he won't settle. Do you have any ideas to calm him?

Temper-Tossed

If I did, I'd be nominated by parents everywhere for a Nobel Peace Prize. Alas, to paraphrase Dr. McCoy from the old television series *Star Trek*, "I'm a doctor, not a miracle worker." In truth, getting your son to quit his fit is not as unlikely as you might think. It's just not as instant as you might like.

The primary purpose of discipline is to teach a lesson. To oversimplify a bit, we say to children, "If you do *x*, I'll do *y*." Discipline is a promise of predictability. It shows children that they will be held responsible for their conduct, even if they don't cease that conduct in a timely manner.

A secondary purpose of discipline is control. Initially grown-ups attempt to control children's behavior so that eventually the children will come to control themselves. In other words, external controls and consequences eventually teach internal restraint.

Teaching a lesson happens immediately. Teaching self-control takes years—in some cases, a lifetime. As soon as you tell your son, "Flare, for this fit you're in the corner; keep going, and you're in bed," you've conveyed the primary purpose of discipline. You've taught the lesson.

But just because you've informed Flare of impending reality doesn't mean he'll abruptly change his emotional direction and confess, "I'm so sorry, Mother. Thank you for talking sense into me. The threat of an early bedtime was just the impetus I needed to get hold of myself. Otherwise, I don't know when I would have shut down. Possibly next week."

The lesson is now. The self-control comes later, the result of many lessons.

No, the lesson is now. The self-control comes later, the result of many lessons. Forty-three outbursts from the present one, Flare may ever-so-slowly begin to realize, *Gee, every time I have a blowout, things happen to me that I don't like. I'd better get a quicker grip.* Thus begin the seeds of self-control, of the ability to short-circuit an outburst in progress, and sometimes even before it starts.

Part of your son's seeming imperviousness to discipline is due to a quality he shares with all humans of any age: Once we're on an emotional roll, we more often come to a skidding halt rather than a right-now dead stop. So when children are in a let-it-all-out frustration reaction, not too much will instantly, successfully penetrate their thinking.

By its very essence, an emotional tirade is long on feelings and short on reason. It is during those in-between periods of calm—hopefully far longer than the storms—when the learning has time to sink in, and thus slowly to eradicate the fits.

Also, never underestimate the power of temperament. Some kids by nature are more fiery than others. That is just a fact of their wiring. For them to bring their outbursts under control is a longer, more discipline-involved process. Where Serena can quiet herself at the mere mention of discipline, Blaise practically feeds on punishment as a necessary fuel for his fire. Rest assured, even the most intense of kids can mature at the hands of a strong parent.

In the end, remember, no matter how good the lesson, or how many repetitions, all humans retain the proclivity to throw a fit. The form may change, but not the motive: *I'm mad about what's happening here. And don't try to stop me just yet.*

Bedtime Bad Times

Dear Dr. Ray,

Our four-year-old daughter fights going to bed nearly every night. We are exhausted and to the point where we allow her to stay up as long as she wants. Help!

No Good Nights

The word "fight" means different things to different kids. To Eve, a bedtime fight means lying in bed nagging and whining until either you or she wears down. To Dawn, bedtime is not a real fight until she has to be pushed into the bedroom with a bulldozer, only to chew her way out through the wall six minutes later.

Since bedtime battlers fall on a continuum from soft to

hard core, we'll cover strategies to deal with the whole range. Let's start with how to quiet the Eves of this world. Then we'll see how to lay to rest the Dawns.

Just what is it about sleep that arouses kids so much? Some don't want to miss a thing; they know the real fun starts after they're in bed. Others consider nighttime boring; they just sleep through it. Still others don't want to be apart from the folks—really.

> **Just what is it about sleep that arouses kids so much? Some don't want to miss a thing; they know the real fun starts after they're in bed.**

The most straightforward approach to easing bedtime bad times is to reexamine Eve's bedtime. Like adults, kids need differing amounts of sleep— unfortunately, none need nineteen hours. It may be that pushing your daughter's bedtime back one half hour or so would put it more in "sync" with her biological clock, making her more ready to wind down and less ready to battle. Of course, if she's a quartz model and doesn't slow until 3:00 A.M., there are limits to your flexible bedtime.

Bedtime rituals also can help to ease kids into sleep. Brush teeth together; tell each other a story; ask your daughter what she'd like to dream about; say prayers together; talk about the chocolate cake you're having for breakfast (just kidding). In essence, you're pairing good time with bedtime. Some kids will actually tolerate, even enjoy, going to bed if it means getting your undivided attention for ten to fifteen minutes prior. I once knew a kid who begged for morning and afternoon naps just to have a chance to repeat the nightly routine.

The above ideas won't work for all kids. Sometimes all the savvy parenting in the world can't circumvent the need for firmness. Let's say that little Petula battles bedtime mostly through words and whining. She nags for twelve drinks of water, begs for six bathroom trips, complains about the position of her stuffed animals, and pleads for every known relative to rescue her.

Seldom will she leave her room, however. She may wander over to the doorway, but she won't venture out. Thus, she can still be considered in the "mild resister" range. (I know, that's easy for me to say; I live in another state.)

To quiet her nightly monologue, work at becoming oblivious to it. No matter how much she drones, don't go near the bedroom. There's no way she can be afraid of the dark. Two 650-watt floodlights are illuminating her room and half the backyard. Seven deadbolt locks anchor the closet door; no monster could ever get out of that closet. A fifty-five-gallon drum of juice is sitting next to her bed, with a port-a-john beside that. She could live up there for six weeks if she had to.

So what happens the first night you don't answer her pleas? After forty-five minutes of nonstop wailing, Petula checks her watch. "Hmm, 9:15, where's Mom? She's usually up here ten or twelve times by now. Oh well, I'd better start knocking stuff off the dresser."

Stand firm. Get out of earshot if you have to. Turn up the television. Crawl under the basement steps. Park the car at the end of the street and take a nap in the back seat. But don't give in. Even if you answer only once every six nights, you'll just prolong Petula's stamina. No question, it's hard to be resolute. It's even harder to battle at bedtime every night.

There's a bright side to hearing your daughter ceaselessly plead, "Let me stay up later." At least she's at home. Twelve years from now, she won't be home when she calls you ceaselessly pleading, "Let me stay out later."

Now on to laying to rest the hard-core sleep-shunners. "Hard-core" is defined as any child who will not remain in his bedroom, who crawls out his window and back through yours, or who chews through his floor and drops into the family room.

A passive approach is the ghost tactic. If Casper isn't at least floating around in his room by the appointed hour, he becomes a ghost. No speaking to him; no answering his questions; no television; no toys; no food. He effectively does not exist.

Your goal is to make staying up

> **"Hard-core" is defined as any child who will not remain in his bedroom, who crawls out his window and back through yours, or who chews through his floor and drops into the family room.**

absolutely no fun. Most kids will tire of such status and fall asleep, on the couch, kitchen floor, even in their own beds. If Casper dramatically tries to grab your attention, say, through diving into the refrigerator and devouring tomorrow night's dessert, you have to act. But if you can master the art of acting without talking, this strategy may eventually succeed.

If the ghost tactic isn't appealing, sometimes very firmly placing a youngster back in bed will show her you mean business and that this affair is over. Some parents add a swat on the seat for good measure.

One mother with a steel-willed bed battler told me she installed a screen door on her son's bedroom that could be locked from the hall side. From her descriptions of the little guy, though, I think mere wire mesh would have only made him mad.

You might inform your daughter that if she leaves her room after bedtime, there will be a cost. For example, she will lose tomorrow's cartoons, or a day's worth of her favorite doll—you know, the one that *realistically* closes its eyes as soon as you lay it flat. The cost is up to you and what would work best with your daughter. The key is to pick something and follow through with it tomorrow.

The last word on bedtime bad times is that eventually kids learn to like sleep. I mean, how many teenagers do you know who would rather wash the car than take a nap? And remember the bright side to bedtime bad times. Little Dawn prefers your company over sleep and thus being unable to have any fun whatsoever.

Meal Ordeals

Dear Dr. Ray,

My four-year-old daughter is a picky eater. Often she refuses to eat anything at all. Mealtime is not pleasant at our home.

Fed Up

Meal ordeals—they rank in the big three of everyday preschool problems, right up there with bedtime bad times and temper tempests. Meal ordeals may be the easiest to resolve, though, as nature is on parents' side. Even the most finicky food-refusers eventually will eat because their bodies tell them to.

If you don't want to wait for hunger to drive your daughter finally to do something drastic, like swallow food, here is a menu of suggestions to help simmer down potential meal melees in your home.

One strategy, usually resorted to out of sheer frustration, is the *Seat-until-you-eat* order, or the "You'll sit-there-until-you-eat-or-at-least-take-one-bite" stand. This approach has a few drawbacks.

I think the major difference between grown-ups and preschoolers involves eating and sleeping. Somewhere between childhood and adulthood we grow to crave both.

One, it may work with some kids, but generally not with those who, as long as you are so upset over their fasting, are determined not to take a single bite until their wedding rehearsal dinner.

Two, you may be forcing yourself to sit and supervise. In other words, you too must seat until they eat. And I'm sure you have better things to do with your time than to stare at a four-year-old mindlessly stirring squash throughout his mashed potatoes.

Three, invariably Cookie will whine and fuss ad nauseam. Isn't it amazing the energy those little buggers have on an empty stomach? Invariably, we don't stay fussless, either. A food fight erupts with our pleading, arguing, and finally threatening to force-feed Cookie intravenously.

All this just prolongs the ordeal. During such standoffs, the only consolation we have is knowing that someday twenty-two years from now, Cookie will have to live with the realization that she once had the chance to eat with reckless abandon and not gain weight, and she let it slip by.

Three more effective, less prolonged solutions to meal melees are these:

1. Set a time when the table will be cleared and the meal will officially be over. Whatever is still edible on Candy's plate, that is, whatever is not a greenish-yellow, unrecognizable semiliquid glue, can be covered with tin foil and placed in the refrigerator. This is her meal to eat if or when she eventually gets hungry.

The decision whether to reheat the meal or not is certainly yours, but for most parents the choice to reserve warm or cold food usually hinges on the temperature of their mood at the time of hearing, "Mom, I'm so hungry my belly is bubbling."

2. While you're occupied with your own food, try to ignore the fact that Grace is not occupied with hers. Resist cajoling ("Mmmm, these carrots taste just like chocolate ice cream"), threats ("Sugar, if you don't at least try your beans, you'll never see another Popsicle in this house"), or bribes ("If you eat two bites of bread, you can leave the table until next Saturday").

It may initially agitate your stomach to stifle the urge to prod your preschooler, but it will help if you fantasize that your daughter is actually eating. Imagine that Grace is gratefully relishing the meal you prepared. You may succeed in tricking your stomach into settling down.

One mom told me she spoke to her son as though he were eating. "Aren't those peppers good? I like them, too!" He must have thought she had slipped a bean, because he actually started eating. I think he felt sorry for her.

3. Absolutely no dessert or snacks (save only highly nutritious ones—broccoli, spinach, tufuti, and the like) will be available later in the meal or evening. The temptation is high to allow Honey a vitamin-fortified, fudge-covered, sugar wafer bar just to get "something" into her, but over time she may learn to shun your nutritious offerings in anticipation of more tasty treats later, especially if she knows you get panicky as her hunger strike stretches into five hours.

Besides, for all you know she may have been munching on roots and berries outside. A lot of preschoolers do. Have your daughter finish her meal—it's still in the refrigerator—before she can enjoy the evening's goodies.

I think the major difference between grown-ups and preschoolers involves eating and sleeping. Somewhere between childhood and adulthood we grow to crave both.

A Separating Peace

Dear Dr. Ray,

Last year my four-year-old son loved preschool. This year he clings to my legs and refuses to leave me. The teacher says he usually settles in about fifteen minutes after I'm gone. What's going on?

Leg Cramps

I don't know, not for sure anyway. But I can take a few educated guesses. After all, that's what a lot of shrinking, and parenting, is about.

Educated guess #1: Something has changed. Because a youngster's life is constantly in flux—new family routine, new siblings, new teachers, new friends—his reaction to life is constantly in flux.

Look around. See what, if anything, might be different for him. Talk with him about the changes, even though they're most likely here to stay. That is, you do plan to keep the new baby, at least until he's fourteen? You don't intend to quit your job, do you, not unless your boss does something you don't like? Indeed, a lot of level living for all ages entails accepting what now is and then moving forward.

Still, if you can find some reason for your son's clinging, you might be able to settle both his and your minds.

Educated guess #2: Nothing has changed, except that your son is carrying on at preschool. More often than not, there is no discernible outside explanation for kids' preschool panic. They're growing up; liking you more—or less; preferring afternoon TV over sitting in circle time; whatever. To put it succinctly, maybe your son has just decided he'd rather not go to preschool, for now anyway.

In response, you have two choices. One, withdraw him—definitely the poorer option. Seldom is it wise to let a four-year-old decide what is in his long-term best interests. Besides, if you pull him out now, how will you know when he's "ready" to return? Typically, the longer kids are away, the less they want to go back.

Choice number two is usually preferable. Your son stays in preschool. My guess (there I go again) is that's what you intended to do anyway. The real question is how to get him to cooperate.

Let's begin with what not to do. Don't try to talk your son into being calm. That's like using kerosene to douse a fire.

"Sweetheart, I'm not leaving for long. I'll be right at home, close to the phone if you need me. Would you look at all those other boys who just love being here with you? Don't you want to play with them? And look at the size of those blocks, your favorite kind, too. Don't you want ..."

All the while the teacher's thinking, "I wonder when the next civil service exam is scheduled."

Cease overreassuring. Walk in the door, pry your son off your leg, kiss him goodbye, with calm firmness hand him over to the teacher, and then leave.

Resist the urge to stare through the window and see how he's doing. He knows you're there; he sees the crowd of other moms.

Resist the urge to stare through the window and see how he's doing. He knows you're there; he sees the crowd of other moms.

When picking him up, focus on the fun he had. Avoid "How did it go?" type questions. Anytime you hear an "I don't want to go to preschool" give a quick "Well, honey, we've got no choice" and then drop it. Or if you prefer, don't respond at all to complaints, nagging, or guilt words.

Are you psychologically damaging your son by "forcing" him to separate for a few hours from the woman he loves more than anyone in the world? No. You are simply making him do something he doesn't want to do, and he's pretty unhappy about that, for ten minutes or so, until he "settles in." Besides, ten years from now you'll be wondering if you're psychologically damaging him by forcing him to be seen in public with you for a few minutes.

As one who specializes in knowing the mind of a child, I often ask, "Who knows the mind of a child?"

Nothing to Toy With

Dear Dr. Ray,

My children are ages six and eight. Getting them to pick up their toys is a daily sore spot in our house. Should I stick to my guns or am I making a mountain out of a molehill?

Day Tripper

Anything that's a daily sore spot may not make mountain status, but it's more than a molehill. Indeed, toy litter is a hot spot in parent-preschooler relationships. It ranks up there with bedtime bad times, meal ordeals, and temper tempests.

Toys are among a child's first possessions. So they offer a natural means to teach responsibility. Unfortunately, responsibility is not something that comes naturally to humans. Like most admirable qualities, it has to be learned.

Why do kids leave coloring books, blocks, and trucks piled waist deep in the family room? (There's your mountain.) Simple: It's easier than picking them up. Besides, they figure they'll just have to get them out again next week, so why make extra work for themselves?

Well, then, why don't they listen when we ask them nicely to play with only twelve toys at a time? Simple: It's easier to ignore us than to pick them up.

Alas, such is basic kidhood. Children generally force themselves to learn about responsibility the hard way (through consequences) rather than the easy way (through words). In a way that's good. Consequences will teach them respect for their possessions, and ours, more quickly and durably than will all the words we can muster.

How might you rid your house of toy clutter—well, at least 75 percent of it? (The only way ever to reach 100 percent is to have no children living with you.) Here are ideas for a nearly litter-free environment.

Get the kids a toy box, or something similar, where toys not in use belong: a shelf, closet, dump truck. Then get yourself a toy box. Every toy you have to pick up goes into your "litter box" and is off-limits for a week.

This little toy rule will drastically reduce nagging ("Morris, how many times do I have to tell you ..."), begging ("Please, Morris, just once, for my sake, gather up your debris ..."), or threatening ("If I pick up one more toy, Morris, you won't have anything new to play with until your kids have toys"). Let your toy box do your talking.

For older kids (spouses, too?) or younger, stubborn ones, you can add meat to your rule by requiring payment of a small fee to purchase the toy back. For example, Mario not only lost his bike for a week because he raced it through the flower-beds again; he also owes you a quarter to get riding privileges back. With teens you can use this fine approach every time you pick up their clothes. After about four days the average adolescent is either penniless or wearing a sackcloth.

Off-limit periods work better when kept short—a few days or a week. By giving Barbie her doll back before the turn of the century, you give her the opportunity to try and try again. If you permanently trash every toy you've picked up over ninety times, you may never face toy litter again, but you've also thrown away the chance to teach Barbie how to care for her possessions. On the other hand, maybe fewer possessions will motivate Barbie to care better for what she has left.

He's done some quick mental arithmetic and figures he could lose a toy a minute until the year 2071 and still only be halfway through last year's Christmas warehouse.

Once your rules go into effect, be prepared for the "I don't care" reaction, conveyed through words or through that familiar mouth wrinkle and shoulder shrug. Ignore it. If Elvis didn't care about losing his ukulele for a week, why would he bother to play with it in the first place?

Then again, maybe Elvis truly doesn't care at first. He's done some quick mental arithmetic and figures he could lose a toy a minute until the year 2071 and still only be halfway through last year's Christmas warehouse. If you persevere, eventually he will care. Even Elvis will get tired of playing with rocks, sticks, and mud balls.

Although, in these days of $120 toy accessories, I think rocks and mud balls will make a comeback.

Wardrobe Wars

Dear Dr. Ray,

My daughter is in the second grade. Every morning we argue over what she'll wear to school.

Worn Out

Kids and clothes—sometimes a real mismatch. Not only will Taylor not put away what she's worn, but she won't wear what we want. With younger children, clothes clashes are the rage on school mornings. The more pressed we are for time, the more frayed a child's tolerance for our choices.

Adolescents follow a broader fashion statement: Parents' clothing tastes evolved during the Mesozoic Era—the early part—and are not to be given twenty-first-century credence.

The fiber of clothes clashes is diverse. Sometimes Calvin simply abhors our combinations. What's attractive to grown-ups often has no appeal to kids. How many eight-year-olds beg to wear a three-piece suit?

Sometimes one particular item of apparel preempts all others, for whatever reason. Maybe a classmate noticed how much Oscar looks like the muppet on his T-shirt pocket. Or maybe a girl in a Corvette commented in passing that Rocky's faded jeans make him look older.

There are several ways to smooth over clothes clashes. You could try on the attitude that whatever Taylor selects is fine with you, so long as it's clean and weather-wise. Plaids with stripes are as acceptable as matching earth tones. Adopting this style will greatly expand your daughter's fashion options while shrinking your frustration.

Some parents are real uneasy allowing a youngster to be a walking advertisement for the new paperback book _Dress for a Mess._

Of course, this approach can test the limits of your self-image. Some parents are real uneasy allowing a youngster to be a walking advertisement for the new paperback book _Dress for a Mess._ If you're among them, a more conservative approach might be to give Taylor a choice of, say, three coordinated outfits. Permitting children some input into their wardrobes often helps iron out disagreements.

One mother laid out her son's school clothes at night. Once agreement was reached, no debates were permitted next morning. If clashes still occurred, the son's bedtime was moved up one half hour that evening. Mom's rationale was that anyone who upsets himself so easily needs more sleep.

There's a bright side to wardrobe wars. They're one sign that Taylor cares how she looks, even if her outfits seem to indicate just the opposite.

School Phobia or What?

Dear Dr. Ray,

In the past month or so, my son (age ten) hasn't wanted to go to school. Almost every morning he says he doesn't feel good. Our family doctor can find nothing physically wrong. And he seems quite healthy at night and on weekends.

Where to Now?

For many years the term "school phobia" was applied to any

child who resisted school for any reason. The assumption was that severe anxiety, if not readily obvious, was lurking somewhere in the depth of the psyche and was at the root of resistance. The thought of leaving home and parents or the thought of school and something about it was so frightening as to be debilitating.

Recently the term has taken on a more narrow meaning. A small percentage of children who resist school can accurately be considered school phobic. The vast majority of school "phobia" is best called school resistance.

The vast majority of school "phobia" is best called school resistance.

Something about attending school bothers or upsets a child. Some anxiety may be involved, but rarely is it the main factor. The reasons behind school resistance are almost as many as kids: not wanting to get up early; boredom with the routine; a change in teachers, grade, or school; an illness resulting in frequent absences; a bus bully; gym. Perhaps most straightforward, being at home means more free time and fun than being at school.

Sometimes a parent can identify the source of the resistance and may even be able to do something about it. An earlier bedtime means less morning sluggishness. Or a brief chat with a bus driver can cue him to intercept a bully.

Just as often, however, you can't figure out what's going on, or if you can, you can't change it. You can't ride the bus to insulate him from a taunting sixth-grader. If you even voiced the thought, he'd really get nervous. A few punches in the back from some bigger kid is far more tolerable than having

Mom on his bus. Isn't it humbling to realize where we some-times fall on a child's list of life's pleasures?

It's also not uncommon for a child who previously liked school to develop a temporary dislike for it. Something has changed, either with school itself or with a youngster's atti-tude, and the distaste evolves into resistance.

Resistance often takes the form of professed sickness, usu-ally involving the stomach, head, or throat, though kids can get pretty creative in their maladies. I recall one first-grader who told his mother that his throat hurt just below his elbow.

Symptoms may be severe enough to prompt at least one visit to the doctor, yet vague enough to be spontaneously cured by late afternoon. Remarkably, the illness almost never flares up on Saturday or Sunday.

Since I know little about your son, I don't know whether he's primarily anxious or resisting. Judging from this problem in general and what you've said, chances are high he's more resisting than anxious. Even if he genuinely were distraught over school, in many ways you would approach the problem similarly. Your first and foremost concern is to keep your son in school. The longer he stays home, the stronger both his resistance and his anxiety become.

The place to begin, though maybe least revealing, is with your son. Explore what might have changed his feelings toward school. Talk to anyone else you think may give you some perspective—a teacher, principal, bus driver, friend, crossing guard. If there is a clear trouble spot and you can influence it, you may smooth things quickly.

On the other hand, most likely the cause will be beyond

your knowledge or influence. You must then move in other directions. How can you lessen your son's resistance to school? Here are several steps:

1. Inform your son that because the doctor has given him a clean bill of health, you will not allow him to stay home. If symptoms emerge such as fever or cold, these are another matter, but don't tell him that. You'd be surprised how closely some kids can mimic common maladies.

Tell him that if he feels ill at school he can ask to see the school nurse, who may allow him to lie down in the clinic. However, you will ask her to call you on any such day and you will then allow, actually require, him to rest in bed or on the couch—without friends, television, or video games nearby—for the remainder of the evening. Should your son in fact be under the weather, the quiet night won't altogether bother him.

If you're not confident in your ability to judge legitimate sickness, or if your son is incredibly convincing, or if you just want another option, move to step two.

2. On any morning that your son claims illness, he will be permitted to stay home—in bed, all day and all evening, with no entertainment other than reading materials. Where to serve his meals is at your discretion. Again, if he truly is feeling bad, he won't totally mind his semi-solitary confinement. If he isn't, bed will quickly become more

unpleasant or boring than he thinks school is.

Additionally, all schoolwork will be made up completely when he is feeling better. Ask the teacher to give extra assignments. After all, your son missed the in-class explanation and will need some extra practice to master the concepts.

One drawback to this approach is that it may take a few days to work. Put another way, it will take however long it takes your son to become convinced that this is the procedure for every "sick" day. A second drawback is that this approach is only practical if you can stay home. If you can't, you might consider making arrangements with a friend, relative, or sitter to supervise for a few days, either at your home or hers. Alas, much of parenthood boils down to logistics.

Two themes run throughout these steps. One, you are making school the more enjoyable of your son's options. Two, your stance is nonnegotiable. No matter how much your son might temporarily hate his scholastic lot, to allow him to avoid it is to allow him to take a course of action the repercussions of which he can't remotely begin to understand.

Car Trouble

Dear Dr. Ray,

Any ideas for managing kids' behavior while in the car? My three children (ages six through twelve) make even the shortest trips miserable for me with their constant bickering, whining, and just overall unpleasantness. The thought of a long trip is terrifying.

Alternative Transportation?

A car is the average American's first choice for transportation. It's the average parent's last choice, if it comes equipped with kids, anyway.

To be perfectly fair to cars, they don't start out on parents' bad sides. Just ask any semicomatose parent of a colicky infant, who knows peace only when endlessly circling the block at 3:00 A.M., with Bliss finally conked out in the car seat. Cars become the seat of family friction about the time kids become old enough to get bored in backseats, ask forty questions per minute with gusts up to sixty, and do vicious things such as look at each other.

Kids feel relatively safe in cars. They know that your discipline options decrease with every mile per hour increase in speed.

In short, kids feel relatively safe in cars. They know that your discipline options decrease with every mile per hour increase in speed. True, they might fear your consequences upon arrival, but several factors keep their fear from curtailing their rowdiness.

One, discipline is literally at some point down the road. The more the miles, the less the deterrent. Two, the kids figure they've got time for you to cool down. That's why they start acting civilized a few hundred yards from journey's end. And three, chances are there will be people where you're headed. Children count on your reluctance to make a scene by disciplining them in front of those other nice people.

Come on, how bad can kids really act in car seats or seat belts? Anybody who asks this is the same kind of person who asks, "How much damage can a little earthquake do?"

In keeping any vehicle running smoothly, preventive

maintenance is a key. Consider keeping a small bag of books, toys, and games in the car to occupy time. Play the alphabet game: Race through the alphabet by finding each letter on signs as you drive. The winner gets to drive—just kidding. Or how about age-appropriate trivia: Name three candy bars that begin with 'M'. What's the most common car color? How far away is that bridge?

Certainly not all disciplinary trouble can be headed off. Therefore, here are four discipline options. Most are based upon a standard discipline law: When you can't discipline, discipline when you can. Meaning, if you aren't able immediately to respond to car trouble, fix the trouble when you do stop.

1. When chauffeuring the kids—to a party, swimming, restaurant, shopping—tell them before departing what level of peace you expect, and that you will turn the car around if you don't get it. Whether you head home for the day, or only for a time before trying again, is your decision, based upon things like the level of car chaos or distance from the house.

What if you previously agreed to transport? Is this going back on your word? I think not. Transportation is a privilege, not a right. Privileges need to be treated well or they are lost.

2. "If you don't stop that right now, I'm going to pull this car over" has been threatened by so many parents in so many cars that it's lost power. And that's too bad, because it's a good option. If you can find a safe place, pull over and sit.

This will idle away valuable time from the kids' swimming, party, or whatever. Require several minutes of quiet before moving on. You can pull over as often as you choose, or simply once, heading for home the second time trouble starts.

3. Deduct travel time. For example, if you endured seventeen minutes of chaos this trip, next trip will be delayed an hour. Don't forget.

Thus far, we've talked about driving where the kids want to go. What if they don't want to go—to school, grocery shopping, a "boring" relative's house, the psychologist? The above rules still apply; the consequences may have to be more delayed.

4. At the start of each trip, the kids get, say, three tickets. Every infraction costs a ticket. Each lost ticket leads to some consequence: ten minutes sitting time, twenty-five sentences written, a twenty-five-cent fine. You could also reverse this and hand out tickets for infractions. Consequences are served upon arrival if possible, or later at home.

If tickets are a hassle, use words: "A.J., every time I say your name, you'll have to do _____ when we get to the _____ or home."

The key to turning off car trouble is to abandon the misperception that to be effective, discipline has to be immediate. This is an ideal state of affairs applicable mainly to toddlers and preschoolers. Discipline fast becomes logistically more complicated as kids get older. That is why it is far better to do something, even if at a later time and place, than to do nothing simply because the moment of nastiness was six miles ago.

If all else fails, you can fall back on a particularly cruel technique. You could tune the radio to your music and sing robustly, proclaiming wistfully, "Now, that's music." You'll probably send the kids into a catatonic state, but don't worry: They'll snap out of it once they escape from the car and tell their friends how bizarre you are.

The Get-Busy Signal

Dear Dr. Ray,

My sons, ages nine and ten, start misbehaving the minute I get on the phone. This makes for some unpleasant phone conversations.

Rung Out

Sometime before his third birthday the typical child figures out when and where his parents' disciplinary options are limited—at the store, in church, visiting permissive relatives, in the car, and on the phone, to mention a popular few. Minivans are maxi-trouble for this reason. No more is Edsel a parental arm's length away, as was the case in passenger cars. Now he can safely act up in the rear seat of a minivan well beyond his parents' reach. And from a kid's perspective, six feet of disciplinary distance in a moving vehicle is comparable to being in the next area code on land.

The phone's ring or the soft sound of your fingers doing the walking are your sons' get-busy signals. Soon their mother will be occupied and less able to respond to their antics.

What's more, kids know that the phone is someone else's ear into our house. No parent likes to sound rattled, so usually we only menacingly wave our free arm while silently mouthing some threat like, "When I'm off this phone ..." Almost always, this has zero effect because the kids have long since calculated to the tenth inch the fully stretched length of the phone's cord, and they're exquisitely careful to create discord just beyond its reach.

To answer your phone disciplinary needs, you can subscribe to two basic plans: A.C.& T. (A Cordless Telephone) or M.C.A. (Make Children Accountable). A cordless phone permits unhindered movement. Your ability to reach out and touch someone anywhere in the house could go far in reducing phone interference.

This plan, of course, has a major disadvantage. Even with full freedom of movement, you're still left with a conference call problem. That is, how do you converse calmly with a caller while simultaneously redirecting your sons?

> Kids know that the phone is someone else's ear into our house. No parent likes to sound rattled, so usually we only menacingly wave our free arm while silently mouthing some threat like, "When I'm off this phone ..."

M.C.A. may be your better option. Its main feature is a rule: From next call forward, whenever Alexander and Watson create static while you're on the phone, they will be placed in chairs or in their rooms for the duration of the call. They'd better hope you don't get call waiting.

This rule means you must be willing to excuse yourself from the phone, even calling back if necessary, to enforce your words. One parent said her children's conduct made her hang up from a long distance call, so she charged them for the callback. Her stand was this: If a child's behavior causes someone inconvenience or expense, the child pays for it through allowances, piggy bank money, or chores.

Should you prefer not to leave the phone, establish post-call consequences. For example, rudeness results in fifteen minutes sitting time. Or fifty-word apologies will be written to you and the caller. Whatever you decide, communicate it before the phone rings again.

Also, practice noticing whenever the boys do allow you to speak in peace. Thank them. Hug them. Tell them that five days of good phone conduct means a half-hour extension of bedtime.

Your sons' phone etiquette will improve as they realize that your willingness to discipline doesn't end when a phone call begins. In the short run, you may be inconvenienced. In the long run, your phone time will be more enjoyable. So will your sons.

Sibling Quibbling

Dear Dr. Ray,

My twin sons are age ten. They bicker and battle about one third of the time they're together. Is this normal, and what can I do about it?

The Referee

To answer your first question: Is it normal for siblings to bicker about one third of their time together? Probably not. In fact, one third sounds a little low. My guess is that typical brothers and sisters wrangle about half the time they're within eyesight.

The experts call your situation "sibling rivalry." For me, that's too psychological. It conveys the impression that the kids are directed by some innate drive to contend with each other, vie for your attention, gain family victory over the other, and overall just move the other out. (I know, sometimes you feel like moving out yourself.)

Sibling quibbling seems the better term. It more clearly conveys what is really going on. Two or more incompletely socialized, partially mature human beings are living together and learning ever so slowly how to get along. Of course, they're going to clash.

Your sons don't seem to bring out the absolute worst in each other. After all, they don't bicker about two thirds of the time. Of course, I'm assuming that this is conscious time. I doubt they bother each other much when they're asleep—both asleep.

At times, the baiting, teasing, arguing, and free-for-all-ing that erupts when sibs get too close to each other ("too close" is defined as "on the same continent") can get so nasty that you wonder

If the saying is true that "you only hurt the ones you love," then the mutual love of some siblings knows no bounds.

whether either feels an ounce of affection for the other. Actually, brothers and sisters can battle heavy and long and still be normal. They may sound scary, but the sibling bond can bend nearly in half before it breaks. If the saying is true that "you only hurt the ones you love," then the mutual love of some siblings knows no bounds.

What breeds all this friction? The reasons are almost as many as kids themselves: sharing parents, rooms, or possessions; competing for perks, privileges, and stuff; breathing the same air; searching for tattle-worthy crimes, serious things like talk-burping, looking at each other, or squirting water through your teeth. Perhaps most simply, some kids just consider their brother or sister a tagalong, pain in their anatomy, who can't wait to run to Mom and "tell" so he can get Brownie points.

If you wonder how much bickering is too much, ask yourself these questions: How often do the kids really fight? Are their quiet times slipping by you unnoticed? It's easy to hear only the noise and not the silence. Are they playing even as they fight? In other words, they can't live with each other but they can't live without each other.

How long has the squabbling been their style? It's not unusual for siblings who were former friends to pass through stretches of weeks, months, or even a few years when they don't seem to have much in common. In good families, maturity works magic. Most kids eventually realize that brother Benedict isn't a total turncoat, bad guy after all.

As normal as sibling quibbling is, that doesn't mean it's right or good. Kids need to learn that brothers and sisters are as worthy of respect as anyone else. Family ties don't excuse nasty treatment. So you need a few ideas to teach respect, or at least limit disrespect.

The first rule: Don't try to figure out who started it. That's only a general rule. Every once in a while you just might have to finger a culprit, like the time Bruno tied Rocky to the trash barrel for pickup. Most of the time, however, playing detective in kid clashes will only result in your ears being assaulted by stereophonic discord at 135 decibels (fifteen above pain threshold).

Rocky: Mom, make him quit looking at me.

Bruno: Why would I ever want to look at you unless I wanted to get sick?

Rocky: You were too, and you burped right on my head.

Bruno: I did not. I faked it. And that's just because you kicked my truck over on purpose.

Rocky: Your truck? Grandma gave that truck to both of us. Besides, I was playing with it until I went to the bathroom.

Bruno: Yea, and you were in there an hour. Who do you think you are—Dad?

Mack (walking in): Did anybody see my truck?

And the beating goes on. You'd have a better chance at working off the national debt than digging to the bottom of one of these interchanges. Instead of trying to ascertain who did what to whom when and with what, establish a few house rules for a fair fight. Since your sons are the same in age and probably size, try these.

> **Instead of trying to ascertain who did what to whom when and with what, establish a few house rules for a fair fight.**

1. Decide what your terms of engagement are. For example, no hitting, shoving, taunting, name calling, jumping off the ropes, or throwing into the crowd.

2. When you do have to intervene, no tattling will be heeded. All parties will receive equal consequences.

3. What are equitable consequences? Here are some favorites of veteran parents of sibling wars.

- Immediate separation. Both boys can sit for a specified time in chairs, on floors, in corners, in rooms, or wherever you choose, and as far from one another as possible. Do you have a second home in Florida?

- If they sit at the same table, neither can get up until each apologizes and gives the other permission to get up. They'll either quickly figure out how to cooperate or they'll rot there until bedtime.

- Both boys can sit back to back for, say, fifteen minutes and neither can leave until they shake hands and part in a truce. Some siblings consider this infinitely worse than separate neutral corners. They usually gag, grumble something about "gross," or "Mom, he's pushing his back against me as hard as he can on purpose."

- Both can write a hundred-word essay on self-control or getting along together. How about letters of apology to each other? Minimum fifty words.

- The TV, bike, game, or whatever was the focus of the fracas can be removed and given to each separately for, say, ten minutes. If, however, the boys can play cooperatively, they can share the disputed object for an hour.

The eventual success of any approach lies in clearly establishing what you will and will not allow between siblings and in using consequences every time to back up your expectations. Kids don't heed each other's words much. Why should they heed yours unless you're willing to act?

There's a bright spot to quelling sibling quibbling. You're forced to hone the skill of dodging dead-end arguments. And that's a skill that's valuable not just with children, but with grown-ups as well.

Sibling Mismatches

Dear Dr. Ray,

My nine-year-old daughter bullies her six-year-old brother. I think he often instigates, but she reacts physically.

Not the Equalizer

Even if your son did start it by teasing, your daughter can't finish it by swinging. If she does, her consequences exceed his.

To reduce your son's subtle needling and your daughter's not-so-subtle reaction, implement a hands-off policy. No one is allowed to get physical, for whatever reason. Even if your son did start it by teasing, your daughter can't finish it by swinging. If she does, her consequences exceed his.

For instance, if he sits for ten minutes to cool down, she sits for twenty. You are effectively putting a heavier price on a physical retort than on a verbal one, and also expecting greater self-control from your daughter, who is older.

The real trick is disciplining when you don't know what happened. Suppose your son has barged into the bathroom—the only true domestic sanctuary—yelling, "Mom, she pushed me and said, 'This is for getting me stuck with that stupid rule.'" Your daughter is two seconds behind countering with, "He said, 'Nah-nah, you're gonna sit longer than me,' and then he fell backwards when I raised my fist, but I never touched him. Honest."

First, consider ordering both out of the bathroom and locking the door. (Why didn't you lock it to begin with?) When you emerge you'll be able to assess the problem more calmly.

Next, call the kids together. Brace yourself for any aftershocks from their earlier quake. Inform your son: "Whenever you tattle on your sister, I will separate both of you." You are making him weigh whether making problems for his sister is worth, say, missing part of a favorite TV show.

Tell your daughter something like "Under no circumstances are you to hit your brother. If you can't learn to ignore his teasing, come and tell me he's bothering you, and I'll try to keep a closer ear on the situation. If that doesn't solve things, you can't go near each other for an hour."

Separation can be highly inconvenient for siblings. One, it interrupts whatever else they were enjoying as they were tormenting each other. And two, it forces them to stay apart, something they won't like doing if they know they have to.

These are not foolproof ideas for eliminating sibling mismatches, but they should reduce it. And that's the real goal with most kinds of rowdy behavior.

Sibling Self-Solutions

Dear Dr. Ray,

What do you think about the standard advice from experts that says, "Stay out of sibling conflicts. Let them work things out themselves"?

Bystander

I think it is misguided, unworkable, and dangerous. Other than that, I believe it has merit.

It is misguided. By their very nature, children are partially socialized and partially moralized human beings. And the younger, the more partially. Indeed, sometimes even with age maturity comes slowly. Some adults remain quite incompletely socialized all their lives. In general, though, the average kid is much less grown up than the average grown-up.

The advice, "Let siblings solve their own clashes," assumes a degree of maturity, or "conflict resolution skills," that few children have. On paper the advice might sound reasonable, even appealing: Let children learn as they go, or more precisely, as they go after each other.

If mutual cooperation came naturally, there wouldn't be so many high-priced motivational speakers trying to teach adults how to interact in a win-win way.

In real life, however, it seldom works that way. Two or more childish beings are likely to flail about, driven by self-interest, toward a resolution where only one wins. If mutual cooperation came naturally, there wouldn't be so many high-priced motivational speakers trying to teach adults how to interact in a win-win way.

The notion is unworkable. Unless your children are comparable in age, size, intellect, feistiness, willfulness, altruism, and on and on, the fight will not be fair. The more dominant child will resolve things in his favor. This is the first lesson in Human Nature 101.

What ten-year-old boy will say to his six-year-old sibling, "OK, let's try to work this out. You are my flesh and blood, so I need to be aware of your needs also, not just my own. Tell you what. You take the game first, and play with it as long as you like. After all, you are younger, and so I should be the one to sacrifice here. I was six once, so I know just how you feel."

If you have a child like this, I agree with the rule: "Let him work it out." In fact, I'd say, "Let him raise himself."

In the world of real kids, self-love is much stronger than sibling love. Only with much time and guidance, by a parent and not a sibling, do children learn to inhibit their self-interest and act cooperatively with others.

The "solve it themselves" advice is dangerous. Even if Harmony and Justice eventually do get good at resolving their disagreements, how much damage will take place in the meantime, as they learn to cooperate via youthful trial and error? How many names called? How much volume, nastiness, and emotional turbulence? Hurt feelings and hurt bodies?

In essence, there will be a whole lot of bad treatment happening on the way to good treatment. The sibling bond is strong and can weather a lot of assault. But that doesn't mean the assault is good or strengthens the bond.

There is one way to help siblings solve it themselves. You set the conditions within which they are permitted to work it all out. For example, your house rule might be: "Any mistreatment of a brother or sister brings discipline." As long as Rocky and Max remain within your terms of engagement, they can learn conflict resolution skills all they want. If they do break your rule, and they will often—they're only partially socialized, remember—you will intervene as you see best, disciplining one party or all parties involved.

Teaching children how to treat each other with kindness and respect is not a brother or sister's job. It is ours. True, they do learn some from each other. But the prime socializer of a child is a parent, not another child. You are much better at being a parent than they are, despite what they may sometimes think.

Labor Relations With Children

Dear Dr. Ray:

How important do you think it is for children to help around the house? And how can I get my kids to do more? Sometimes it's easier on my nerves if I just do the chores myself.

Working Mother

Chores are loaded with lessons about life. They show, not merely tell, a youngster that living in this home is everyone's privilege, so it is everyone's responsibility. Chores foster a sense of shared ownership, and as such a respect for property, their own and another's.

Household duties are forerunners of lessons about the

work world. They help a child understand that work is insepa-
rable from life, not just for grown-ups, but to a lesser degree,
for those growing up.

The most durable lessons are taught young. Introduce kids
to chores early, before they become allergic to work and sweat.
Little ones love to help out, especially if they think chores are
something reserved only for big people.

Take full advantage of toddlers' drive to imitate. Work in
the same room together. Give them their own rag to help wipe
the table, or dust, or dry their drinking cup. Let them hold
onto the vacuum while you sweep. Odds are good they'll mess
more than they clean, but you're nurturing a good attitude in
them: *I have to help, too.*

Preschoolers are quite capable of doing their share. Two-
year-olds can put away puzzles, toss their cup into the sink.
Three-year-olds can help set the table, put clothes where they
belong, control toy debris, and keep play areas within the city
health code.

In the beginning stages of teaching chores, much of the
effort is yours, but it's effort aimed at the future. As with any
behavior, a little work on the front end of parenthood will pay
off handsomely in coming years. As a child internalizes some
sense of responsibility, the need for parental prodding
decreases.

Joint ventures are a good option. One mother said, "The
kids will give me twice the help if we do chores together, rather
than my giving them separate work." For example, you wash
the dishes and they dry. Or they wash and dry, but you straighten
the kitchen. Sometimes merely puttering nearby, even if

you're faking looking busy, weakens the kids' conviction that you're the straw boss and they're the slaves.

Certainly this doesn't mean that for every job you ask of John Henry, you must share the experience. Contrary to his impression, you do have other demands on your time. Then, too, some things should be his sole responsibility. On the whole, however, timing your work to coincide with his should improve his output.

Shared chores offer an unexpected bonus. The "forced" togetherness can prompt children to open up with their thoughts and feelings. High-quality conversations often are spontaneously wrapped around a cooperative leaf raking or housecleaning. Chores are prime times for kids to talk to us, even if it's just because we're the only ones around.

Even if most kids' present workload were doubled, the burden would still only entail about a one-hour workweek.

Sometimes parents ask little of kids, saying there's little for them to do. My advice is to find things for them to do, or make them up. The typical youngster is far from over-houseworked and would greatly benefit by being required to do more. Even if most kids' present workload were doubled, the burden would still only entail about a one-hour workweek.

Quite naturally, as kids get older more activities compete with their time and desire to work for or with you. Therefore, you may need to structure your expectations. You may need some strategies for making children's chores less work for you than for them.

Since household duties are standard requirements, or

should be, in most homes, they are standard sources of friction. Typically kids want to do less than we'd like. And if our main means of eliciting their help is through nagging, threatening, and yelling, then truly it would be easier for us to do their chores—if not on our muscles, then on our minds.

The following are some ideas for making your youngster's chores less work for you, while cutting back on the emotional turbulence that can drag a four-minute job into a forty-minute tug of word-war.

1. Make a list of household duties you would like from your kids. For most parents, the "would like" list is much longer than the "getting done" list. Divide this list into family chores—those chores that are expected because a child is a member of the family—and pay chores—those chores that will be linked to an allowance.

If pay chores aren't completed in a timely fashion (*you* define "timely," not the kids), allowance money is proportionately deducted. The motivating power of this approach depends upon two key elements: One, provide *no* money for extras during any week when all chores aren't completed. Two, if children earn money independently (through baby-sitting, lawn mowing, birthday card opening, or whatever), require a higher percentage to be saved—for instance, 75 percent as opposed to 50 percent—during any period in which they have not earned all their allowance.

> **Establish a core chore rule: All daily duties must be complete before privileges begin.**

2. Establish a core chore rule: All daily duties must be complete before privileges begin. If room-cleaning day is Wednesday, then no TV, phone, outside air, toys, or fun with friends are available until the room has been mucked out and fumigated.

3. For Saturday duties, or once-a-week chores, construct a list. Let each child alternatively select from the list, for a fair chance at the easier jobs.

4. For younger children, construct a chore wheel. List household tasks or rooms to be cleaned, and everyone spins the wheel for an assigned task until all have been "won." Variants of a chore wheel include flipping a coin to decide who washes the dishes and who dries, pulling chore duties out of a jar, or tossing a Velcro ball at a chore chart.

This last one should bring out any hidden athletic ability in the kids. They'll learn to hit the one-inch square marked "Wipe the bathroom sink" from sixty feet while never touching the two-foot poster of "Scrub the kitchen floor."

5. When duties are alternated—that is, one time Hazel vacuums, the next time Alfred does—to insure a cleaner performance, establish that any job needing to be redone results in an earning of the next turn. You may have to monitor to make sure that three minutes after Hazel has meticulously vacuumed the family room, Alfred doesn't sneak in and sprinkle cookie crumbs under the coffee table.

Technology makes less work for everyone. There's not as much need for children to help as there used to be. Consequently, we may have to work a little harder to identify ways for them to share the load. It will be to our short-term and their long-term advantage.

Underachievement—School Problem #1

Dear Dr. Ray,

My son is eleven years old. His teacher says he is quite capable of doing his schoolwork, but his grades are very poor. He seems to lack initiative. Is this a common problem? And what can I do to motivate him?

Tired of Pushing

Yours is by far the most frequent school-related question I receive from parents. In sheer numbers, underachievement—a child's not working up to potential—dwarfs the incidence of other, more highly publicized school problems such as school phobia and Attention Deficit Hyperactivity Disorder.

Before we try to motivate the undermotivated, one caution is needed. Some children who look like underachievers really aren't. Intellectual or learning problems underlie their school struggles. Likewise, life troubles can temporarily cause a child to push schoolwork into the background. These factors need to be ruled out through consultation with teachers or psychologists before concluding that a youngster is truly capable of more than he or she is showing.

Still, in the majority of cases, kids who perform poorly in school are not hindered by learning or other problems. They are quite able to do their work, often at an above-average level. These are the youngsters we will talk about now.

Typically, the underachievement pattern has been forming for at least several months, if not several years. Resistance to schoolwork began back in the early grades and motivation has continued to wax and wane ever since. Assignments are regularly left unfinished during class time. Homework routinely stays at school or is lost, left in the bushes, "forgotten," eaten by the dog, or lied about. "Honest, Mom, this is the third teacher I've had since second grade who doesn't believe in homework or tests!"

Underachievers are the ones to whom many parents refer when lamenting, "We've tried everything; nothing works."

Underachieving youngsters seem to spend most of their scholastic energy finding ways to skirt schoolwork. Every so often an internal fire flares—usually during the early stages of some new system we're trying—but exasperatingly the fire is short-lived.

Underachieving children completely frustrate parents and teachers. They resist encouragement, rewards, and punishment. Standard discipline is usually ineffective because little is powerful enough consistently to overcome such children's distaste for schoolwork. In short, underachievers are the ones to whom many parents refer when lamenting, "We've tried everything; nothing works."

What drives certain kids to be so undriven? Some downright dislike schoolwork. To them, it is boring, frustrating, or meaningless. They see little purpose in it and would much prefer occupying their school day with more immediately enjoyable pursuits, such as counting cars passing on the road outside, reassembling their pen each minute, or watching their favorite daydreams playing on the ceiling.

Other children have subtle delays in such areas as maturity or concentration. Nothing is severe enough to warrant special services; overall, these kids are still able to do the work. They just have to concentrate harder or spend a little more time at it. Consequently, some of them take the initially easier route and gradually quit trying.

As seemingly stubborn a problem as underachievement is, it responds rather well to one particular approach. It's an approach that is elegantly simple, and perhaps more importantly, unbeatable. Even little Newton, as creative as he is, won't be able to find loopholes in it. Let's call it the "note home procedure." Here's what to do.

1. *Obtain a small spiral notepad.* This pad will be your youngster's constant school companion. Require him to carry it to and from school every day. Actually, any kind of record sheet will do. The advantage to a pad is that it's small and holds a lot of pages, thus allowing you more easily to look back, measure progress, or see patterns.

2. *Keep a daily record.* At the end of each school day, or each period if need be, Oxford is to list in his pad all homework assignments, incomplete classwork, failed tests, and anything else you would like included. If he is too young to keep his

own record, in my experience most elementary teachers are quite willing to note everything that needs to be completed or redone.

3. *Ensure accuracy.* Obviously, a teacher-completed pad must be assumed accurate. If Webster fills out his own pad, he has the added responsibility of asking his teacher to initial it each day. The teacher gives initials if, *and only if,* everything is listed correctly. If not, the teacher offers neither corrections nor initials. On any day that Webster has finished all work at school, he writes, "All work is done," and seeks the confirming initials.

4. *Schoolwork is completed immediately after school.* Set up a quiet, isolated spot at home where all schoolwork can be finished. Only when schoolwork is completed—correctly—can privileges and activities begin. Not until then. Schoolwork is the evening's first order of business.

Shouldn't Holmes be given a "break" after school to unwind before beginning to work? I don't think so. He had his break at school. He didn't do much for six hours.

5. *The pad is the ticket to privileges.* Without the assignment pad, Holmes does not earn evening privileges. The pad is the ticket to television, stereo, phone, games, outdoors—in short, everything but breathing, eating, bathroom, and of course, reading.

What if the pad comes home without initials or without all necessary books? This is where the procedure most often unravels, and kids know it. They are incredibly resourceful at conjuring up explanations for a missing or incomplete pad:

"We had a substitute today, and he said he doesn't sign anything without his lawyer reading it first." "That big bully, Butkus, made me eat the paper because he knew I'd get in trouble."

No matter what the reason, even if possibly legitimate, that pad *must come home, signed and with books.* It is unquestionably your youngster's full responsibility. Try to validate every excuse you hear, and you're forcing yourself into a guessing game where facts are few.

If you don't want to curtail all evening's privileges, you have another option, in some respects a better one. Beg, borrow, or buy a copy of all your son's books to keep at home. If you can't get them, get something similar on his grade level from a local bookstore. Then, if any subjects are in question, you give assignments from your books, and make sure your assignments are longer than anything he would ever have gotten at school. Your goal is to show him it is definitely in his best interests to bring home all books and work.

School is the work of children. In effect, you are making a statement: At age eleven, you do not have free choice to do or not to do your schoolwork.

6. *Persevere.* The note home procedure most likely won't work quickly. It may takes weeks, months, or even all year. For the first twenty-two days, Patience might play with her pencil and study the ceiling until 7:00 P.M. Persist. A habit as long-standing as underachievement doesn't pass quickly, no matter how consistent your methods.

To add effectiveness to the note home procedure, keep several points in mind.

- This approach is meant to be clear-cut and no-nonsense. Your stance is nonnegotiable. Where your youngster's academic skills are concerned, you cannot afford to be irresolute. School is the work of children. It is their future. In effect, you are making a statement: At age eleven, you do not have free choice to do or not to do your schoolwork.

- The note home will not immediately put schoolwork on Stanford's list of favorite things. It does not internally motivate him. It is pure external motivation. With time Stanford will develop personal motivation, because he'll see success, and that will change his self-image as an underachiever. Until then, you will be making him keep abreast of his work and learn the skills he'll need when he finally does decide to push himself.

- Do not hover over, prod, threaten, debate, or nag Stanford to complete his work. The problem is not yours. You have no reason to feel guilty. Help when you feel necessary, but otherwise let the approach do your talking.

  Stanford is fully aware what the ground rules are. If he makes his life less pleasurable for a while, that is his choice. He is not foolish. He will motivate himself when he tires of his chosen lifestyle.

- Set positive goals. For example, if Watson completes all classwork at school for three days in a row, he can earn a bedtime extension. Gradually lengthen the requirements.

The note home procedure is virtually foolproof if you stay with it. Once your youngster is convinced it's part of your house routine, he will work to make it unnecessary. In so doing, he will no longer underachieve.

After-School Discipline

Dear Dr. Ray,

My son, age ten, misbehaves a lot in class. The school psychologist says it's a behavior problem and that we need to work with his teacher. But how? He's in school and we're at home.

Absent From School

A core law of school life: Parents have far more authority than teachers. Therefore, in affecting how a youngster acts in class, a parent can be more influential, even though the teacher is more immediately present.

High in the ranks of parental frustration is the weekly, sometimes daily, wait for the school's call reiterating young Stanford's latest piece of recalcitrance. Compounding the exasperation is the sense of impotence at being four miles away and three hours past when the trouble occurred. And rowdy kids are well aware of that time-space reality. Indeed, they gauge their impulses by it. You are out of sight, out of mind, and out of range.

So how do you project your authority into your son's classroom? Rest assured, it can be done.

Step one: Meet with the teacher. I know, you've already had sixteen meetings. You talk with the teacher, it seems, more than with your spouse. But meet once more to set up a potent, kid-proof behavior plan.

Step two: Design a rating system. Using a spiral pad, note card, laminated sheet, whatever your preference, lay out four descriptions: Excellent, Good, Fair, Poor. Each day the teacher is to check or circle the rating that best summarizes your son's level of cooperation in class.

Some teachers simply use E-G-F-P. For young children, a series of smiling to frowning faces can define the progression. Absolutely critical is that a rating must come home every day accompanied by the teacher's signature or initials. Otherwise, no matter what, the day is automatically a "Poor." Few kids will hide or forget to bring home an Excellent or Good.

Step three: Determine what behavior leads to what rating. For example: Two problems or less result in an "Excellent." Three or four earn a "Good." Five bring on a "Fair." More than five episodes represent a "Poor" day. In addition, one big piece of trouble, say, disrespect to the teacher, could automatically rate a "Poor."

Make the rules specific and clear-cut—for example, no leaving seat without permission, no arguing, no teasing. Any infraction of a rule immediately earns a tally. Your ultimate goal, usually reachable within a month or so, is to fine-tune the system so that zero misbehaviors = "Excellent," one = "Good," two = "Fair," three or more = "Poor."

Step four: Attach home consequences to each rating. An "Excellent" might push bedtime back fifteen minutes, or allow an extra dessert. A "Good" results in normal evening privileges—no more, no less. "Fair" means earlier bedtime and no television. "Poor" wipes out all evening privileges of any kind, as well as leads to early bedtime.

The power in this approach lies in its linkage. Your authority is now directly backing the teacher's. You will act each and every day, decisively, to teach your son to behave well toward all.

How long is the system in effect? Until you decide your son can act well in school without it. The power in this approach lies in its linkage. Home and school are bound together. Your authority is now directly backing the teacher's. You will act each and every day, decisively, to teach your son to behave well toward all.

On my son's first day of kindergarten, I advised him, "Andrew, if you get into trouble, before you leave school today, give your teacher a big kiss and thank her. Because whatever she did to you will be the least of your worries."

A Kid's Room: No Place for a House

Dear Dr. Ray,

Any suggestions for getting kids to keep their rooms halfway livable? My children are eleven and fourteen, and their standard comeback is "It's my room. Why can't I keep it the way I want?"

It's My House

Here are some parents' descriptions of their kids' rooms: "I'm afraid to go in there without a wilderness survival kit and an oxygen mask." "Two of her sisters accidentally stumbled into her bedroom about a year ago and were never seen again." "We call his room *Star Trek*—to venture in is to 'boldly go where no mom has gone before.'"

As creatively as parents can depict the messy room problem, so too can they relieve it. One mother said in a final fit of frustration that she gathered up all the debris decomposing on her son's floor and piled it on the bed—the mound hit the ceiling. Undaunted, her son slept on his newly discovered floor the next three nights. He finally did get the message, and began to sort through the stack. Maybe he needed his sweatpants, buried somewhere near the bottom.

Another parent said that during a cleaning frenzy, he threw every item clogging up his son's bedroom out the front window. Upon returning from school, his son saw the shrubs wearing his gym shorts and tank tops. To paraphrase an old saying, one picture is worth a thousand naggings. Things were borderline straightened out after that.

Dramatic reactions like these can work, but they tend to be short-lived. After the fury has subsided, Comfort's room slowly returns to its prehabitable state. Besides, the initial cleaning is done by the parent, not the child.

More durable solutions to ruined rooms are available. First, decide how you want to view your kids' rooms. (I know— from three miles away.) Parental philosophy here is divided into two camps.

Some consider youngsters' rooms their domain. As long as the door is shut—ideally, a steel-encased door with a twelve-inch external dead bolt—the room is out of sight and out of mind. Other parents believe youngsters' rooms are theirs only up to a point. That is, "It's their room, but it's my house, and I don't want part of my house in violation of the city health code."

Whichever philosophy you prefer determines what action you'll take. The "closed door" tack requires less effort. Basically, the room just exists, and you count on Sandy eventually to develop some desire to keep his turf presentable. Sometimes this happens; other times it doesn't until a youngster has his own place.

In the latter case, here are added suggestions: Do not enter the room to pick up clothes, bed sheets, or other items that need your laundry, tailoring, or general parent service. Sandy can 1) bring the clothes to the laundry room himself; 2) wash all washables himself; 3) repair and mend his own possessions. This is the price tag for keeping the room the way he wants it.

> "It's their room, but it's my house, and I don't want part of my house in violation of the city health code."

The "it's their room, but it's my house" mentality takes more of your energy, but it usually results in a better-kept room. First step: Set up room inspection times, say 6:30 P.M. on Wednesday and 11:00 A.M. on Saturday. If conditions initially are too deplorable, you might want to set up daily, maybe hourly, inspections.

Second step: Decide what the cost will be for a messy room. "Messy" is one of those loose terms that kids like to argue about, so maybe you'd best clearly define "messy" or "unlivable" or "trashed."

Some standard costs could be these:

- No leaving the room until it is cleaned.
- No privileges until the room is cleaned. These could include telephone, television, stereo, car keys, outside play—in some combination or in total. The decision is yours.
- Money can be deducted from Penny's allowance for an unkempt room. If you want to plunge in to sweep and fumigate, you can charge for your time. And you're union scale, aren't you?
- Periodically, link the chance to leave the house to a clean room. For example, if Murdoch asks to go to Igor's birthday party, you might reply, "Sure. If your room is clean." There are enough places he wants to go that you could probably use this kind of linkage daily if need be.

There's a bright side to living near a kid's room. If you run out of storage space in your garage or shed, you can always park the lawn tractor in his room. He'll never know it's there.

For Whom the Bells Toll

Dear Dr. Ray,

My fifteen-year-old is addicted to the telephone. Even with our fifteen-minute maximum rule, she gives and receives so many calls that the phone can be tied up for hours. And her eleven-year-old brother has started to fight for his share of line time.

Always Busy

The telephone—a youngster's life link to the outside world, where the action is really happening. Without a phone, how can Belle know if Alexandra really did tell Watson that she broke up with him because he never called? How can Rocky get the up-to-the-minute scoop on that new substitute teacher who somebody said once played drums for Paula Abdul? (For those of you my age, I think she's a rock star who used to sing with Ringo Starr.)

In so many words, to an adolescent the telephone is the medium to relive and retalk in gripping detail every single minute of the day—the same day about which she said "nothing" when you asked her, "What happened in school today?"

The telephone is more than a means to communicate. It is a social magnet, pulling in today's friends and yesterday's acquaintances who will be tomorrow's best friends. It is a convenient and safe forum for young, playful friendship rituals. It is a diversion from the "routine" of family life. Because its appeal is enormous, its potential for abuse is enormous.

For all these reasons, parents regularly have to decree phone limits because the average child won't. Come to think of it, if kids would just think more like parents, we wouldn't have to do half of the things that make them so mad at us.

There are many reasons to keep your phone lines open. One, people can actually reach you if they need to, or if they just want to. Two, you can reach your daughter more easily. If the phone isn't glued to her ear, she may actually consider telling you about the new substitute teacher who played drums for Paula Abdul. (Parenting Tip #308: Pretend you know who Paula Abdul is, and then look it up later.) Three, she won't gabble up large chunks of phone time, to the exclusion of other good things such as studying, chores, hanging around, or fighting with her brother.

To relieve phone fights, some parents get the kids their own phone. In most cases, this just adds problems. First, it opens the lines to longer occupation. Second, who pays for this privilege? Third, will siblings get their own? Fourth, will you ever see your child in person again? You could call her, if you can get through. Maybe you can get her call waiting.

Speaking of call waiting, some parents go this route. But again, what does it teach? It essentially says, "Go ahead, talk on with your ninety-seven friends, but let me know if any of my three friends calls." Does the child pay? She should, if her phone habit is the reason for the perk. Also, how can you know if someone is trying to get through? I mean, can you actually expect your daughter to cut her commentary, cold turkey, about the kid on the bus who wears a tie just because her father could be stranded in the rain with a dead car battery?

The phone is a privilege, not an entitlement. And a privilege needs to be handled with care, or else it is gone for a while. Here are three ideas for opening up your phone lines.

1. Keep your fifteen-minute limit, but fine-tune it. How about a fifteen-minute limit with a three-call maximum per night? How about a second "time's up" reminder leads to loss of a call? The biggest complication to call limiting is the secondary conversations that can occur with each call.

Us: "Time's up, Polly."

Polly: "In a minute. I just need to help Fulbright solve this last trigonometry problem." (Right.)

Us (three minutes later): "Let's go. Off. Now."

Polly (silently mouthing, "OK, OK"): "Then he said what? Get out. No way."

Us (two minutes later—on the extension): "Polly, I need the phone."

Polly (four minutes later, hanging up): "I can't believe you act like that in front of my friends."

2. To avoid this kind of exchange, how about a house rule: Calls can be accepted only between 4:00 and 4:30 P.M., and 8:00 and 8:30 P.M. Or whatever times you choose. Polly is responsible for sending out a press release to all her friends informing them of the new limited line policy.

What happens if you're not home and Polly decides to tie up the phone lines? Inform her that if you call and it's busy, she will lose the next night's phone privileges. In reply to which you'll soon hear, "I was only on for ten seconds telling Oral to call back at 8:00 because I can't talk now."

To avoid this, call twice, about one minute apart. Two busy signals means Polly isn't listening, to you anyway. Of course, then you'll hear, "Another friend called, and I had to tell her to call back ..."

3. Phone time can be earned. Completed chores lead to x minutes of phone time. Or the lines don't open until all schoolwork is complete and correct. Or extra phone time can be purchased. The money goes to church, a charity, family vacation fund, the phone bill, whatever.

One mother solved most of her phone problems with a radical move. There was only one phone in the house. It was in the kitchen.

When the kids were on it, sometimes Mom left the area, sometimes she didn't. The phone is not so appealing without privacy. The calls were shorter. The content was pretty benign. The kids weren't in full favor of the arrangement, but they lived with it, and it saved a lot of hassles.

Please write in a few weeks to let me know how things are working. Better yet, call. But call after midnight. My daughter is usually in bed then, and you'll have a much better chance of getting through.

All's Fair in Love, War, and Curfews

Dear Dr. Ray,

My teenagers are fourteen and sixteen. We disagree constantly over curfew times. Any suggestions for establishing reasonable limits? And how can I ensure they'll be followed?

The Timekeeper

Let me begin with a safe assumption: Your idea of a fair curfew is earlier than your teens' and not the other way around. I did read once about a fifteen-year-old who argued for an earlier curfew than his parents had set. Last I heard, he was being studied at a leading university's center for unearthly phenomenon.

Actually, parents and teens more often than not agree on what is a reasonable time to be home. We simply talk in different time zones. We parents can live with a midnight curfew, and so can the kids, but we're talking midnight Eastern Standard Time and they're talking midnight Pacific Time (translation: 3:00 A.M. Eastern).

Adolescents want later curfews because they believe, unlike their parents who have lived just a shade longer but who in the kids' eyes are no wiser for it, that they can responsibly handle the liberty of a later curfew. What parent hasn't been met with these words: "Anything we can do at 1:00 in the morning we can do at 1:00 in the afternoon." True. But we oldsters know that the potential for trouble and craziness rises steadily with each minute's journey into the wee morning hours. It isn't so much that we don't trust our kids; it's that we don't trust the others who are out and about at that hour.

Will kids understand your reasoning and willingly accept the curfews behind it? If they do, kiss them once for me. It's not standard teenhood quietly to agree to coming home before they are ready. Teens like being out of the folks' eyeshot and earshot, especially at night. Something about the dark appeals to the independent streak in teens.

Regarding curfew guidelines, begin by seeking the kids' input about what they think is "fair"—that's a four-letter word the teens like to fling around a lot. If you can settle upon mutually agreeable times, you'll probably see more curfew adherence, as the kids have had some say in their limits. If, however, after sixty-two hours of nonstop negotiating through a federal mediator, you and Faith are still three hours apart, you must decide what is fair.

Some families set routine curfews, for example, 9:00 P.M. on weekdays, midnight on weekends. Exceptions are made periodically based on such factors as special occasions, degree of supervision, or Gardiner's promise to mow the lawn for the next seven years without being asked. Or Maybe Faith is double-dating with her boyfriend's parents to the ballet. Right! Curfew here might be extended to 1:30 A.M.

On the other hand, Gardiner wants to use your two-day-old van to take his girlfriend to a quadruple feature at a drive-in somewhere across the state line. In this instance, you might move curfew to 8:00 P.M., one hour before the movie starts.

Some parents have no set curfews, instead judging each request on its merits or lack of. This can work, but it carries more risks for arguments, as each evening out can become a rowdy negotiating session.

Whatever approach you take, the curfews you establish depend upon you, your household, your youngsters, and your situation. Resist the temptation to allow a curfew you feel is unwise because you hear "But there's not even enough time to get anything to eat after the game" or "Not a single guy in the whole school will ask me out because I have to be in so early" or "You just don't trust me" or "Come on, Dad, these are different times from when you were growing up."

"Come on, Dad, these are different times from when you were growing up." Indeed they are. All the more reason for curfews.

Regarding this last one, indeed they are. All the more reason for curfews.

Kids will conjure up all manner of curfew commentary. Most of the time this is a sign that you are disagreed with—not unloved, not unrespected, not necessarily even thought unfair, just plain disagreed with. And hasn't that happened many times before, on issues much smaller than curfew?

Now, on to the acid question: How can you insure Faith will live within her curfew? Acid answer: You can't. The ultimate reality of any discipline is that you can never guarantee your youngster will exercise good judgment. Only she can guarantee that. You can do much, however, to make it more likely she will act responsibly.

Obviously, it would be untrusting, not to mention inconvenient, for you to shadow Faith everywhere and escort her home at the appointed hour. Besides, you would stand out conspicuously at any teen gathering. Your jeans aren't faded enough and they don't have anywhere near big enough holes in the pockets. What's worse, you're so out of touch you still believe dance partners should be dancing at least in the same room.

No, with any curfew you're implicitly making a statement of trust: I believe you'll be home when I've asked you to. Should Faith not be home at a "decent hour" (I'm sure she sees nothing decent about it), then she needs to know there are consequences for tardiness. Here are three ideas.

1. Attending football games, dates, sensitivity encounter groups, or whatever, is a privilege. And a privilege abused is a privilege "losed," at least temporarily. A basic house curfew rule might be: Each fifteen minutes late leads to one day of grounding. The days would best be predetermined, preferably Friday or Saturday. Leave the choice up to Dawn, and she'll choose to stay home on Monday afternoon and Wednesday evenings.

Old-fashioned grounding still works well. But it's always amazed me how often we feel we can't live in the same house with that kid for one more minute, and then we turn around and force her to stay home.

2. A more specific curfew rule is this: For every one minute late without a solid, verifiable reason, five minutes will be taken off the time a youngster has to be home next occasion out. You could use any ratio you wish: five minutes late costs fifteen; fifteen costs an hour; ten costs ten.

Using the one-for-five example, let's say that Knight drifts in at 12:36 A.M. with the excuse that the electricity in the gym went out for thirty-six minutes. (Excuse rating: fairly original, too verifiable, overall nice try). So, 36 x 5 = 180 minutes = 3 hours earlier Knight has to be in next time he wants to go somewhere. If normal curfew tomorrow night is midnight, he has to be in by 9:00.

Brace yourself. You're likely to hear something like this: "It's not even worth going out if I have to be in by 9:00." Probably not.

3. Curfew consequences cut both ways. If Faith follows her curfew, conducting herself responsibly while she's out, then periodically it might be wise to relax the limit by one hour or so. Your message is: Responsibility begets freedom.

Whatever curfew consequences you choose, the common denominator is that they are not threats to be flung at retreating backs as they fly out the door. They are preestablished, automatic house rules designed to improve parental supervision and keep peace.

It's always amazed me how often we feel we can't live in the same house with that kid for one more minute, and then we turn around and force her to stay home.

There's a bright side to working out a curfew. Even though it can cause agitation, it will help you sleep better. An adolescent's curfew time, followed closely by the sound of a key in the door, almost always translates into the exact time that a laying-in-bed-wide-awake parent can finally begin to nod off.

Pick Your Battles?

Dear Dr. Ray,

People often advise me, "Pick your battles" with my children, but I'm not sure exactly what that means or how to do it.

Battle-Fatigued

"Pick your battles" has become a parenting mantra among the experts, a sort of cliché, capable of being shaped into all sorts of meanings. Whether it's good for your child rearing or not depends upon how you apply it.

At one level, I wholeheartedly agree with picking your battles. Much of what any child does that irks a parent is not wrong. It is not moral misconduct, hurtful, defiant, dangerous, or irresponsible. It is kid junk, the stuff of childishness.

Let's say it is little Eve's bedtime. She complies without incident, but while in bed, she softly talks to herself, or lies at the foot of her bed, or makes up a hand puppet play. She's not being bad or unruly; she's just adding her own brand of kidhood to make a bad situation (that is, bed) better.

Perhaps, however, her creativity gets enthusiastic enough to wake up her baby brother. So, you tell her to settle, and she doesn't. Now you have to act. The battlefront has moved into an area that needs to be defended, and you actively intervene with discipline. In essence, there really was no battle until Eve changed the terms of engagement.

A personal scenario: Sometimes while riding in our van, several of our children, usually the youngest and most tone deaf, decide to sing. In itself, I suppose this would be tolerable, but they all sing different songs, with made-up words, in poor timing, and with gusto, which grates on our ears.

I don't think they're doing anything wrong, at least for the first thirty-six seconds or so. They're just being kids, however bizarre. But if either my wife or I should ask them to tone it down, or to stop so we can converse without screaming, they'd better, not only for our sanity but to show respect. We as parents have a right to put a ceiling on the chaos, little battle or not.

There is one meaning of "pick your battles" that drastically undercuts good parents' trying to raise great kids. It is this: Stand firm on the major moral stuff, but be flexible on the minor moral stuff, especially if your youngster is overall a "pretty good kid."

Suppose your thirteen-year-old son, Sting, wants to attend a rock concert with his buddy, Ringo. You're against it. He's too young; there is no adult supervision; the scene is just too crazy. Now some experts (probably those without thirteen-year-olds) would advise: Find a compromise.

Don't strive for unconditional victory, they would say, because Sting could just resent you or fight back harder. Let him go if he takes a cell phone and checks in with you. Maybe Ringo's dad will go with the boys. Or if the rock concert is out, how about a free trip to three movies of his choice instead? After all, you don't want to be rigid.

Maybe here you do want to be rigid. Your child's character or moral protection is involved; therefore, the battle is real important. OK, by today's standards, the concert is relatively benign. The group, "Kids in Charge," has had only two minor felonies and a pending drug probe. Again, some experts would say, negotiate.

This expert's advice? Where your child's morals are at stake, if someone advises you to pick your battles, ignore him.

A more common conflict: Suppose Rocky constantly torments his sister, Adrian. Since sibling squabbling is "normal," shouldn't you overlook most of it? How about: No punching in the face and no name-calling. Run-of-the-mill torments, such as words, looks, or put-downs, are small-arms fire and can be ignored.

Where your child's morals are at stake, if someone advises you to pick your battles, ignore him.

Wait a minute! Is it wrong or isn't it to mistreat someone? If you think it is, then sibling respect is a battle to pick, and to win, no matter how "small" the wrong.

One last salvo: When you pick your battle, don't battle. Stand confident and strong. Enforce your decisions with love and discipline, not arguing, endless lectures, and nagging. The quicker the "battle" is over, the better for all. And the fewer battles you will confront in the future, as your child learns clearly where the moral line is drawn.

Statute of Limitations

Dear Dr. Ray,

I just found out that my nine-year-old stole a box of pens from school over two months ago. Would it do any good to do anything about it now?

Time's Up?

Picture this scenario: You're in traffic court for a speeding offense. The judge says, "You were clocked at seventy-six in a fifty-five mile-per-hour zone. Because I've been on vacation and the docket is backed up, it's been six weeks since you did this. Therefore, case dismissed, but consider yourself lucky I didn't find out about this last week." Think it'll ever happen?

One brand of child rearing theory says: To be effective, discipline must be immediate. In other words, the consequences must follow the crime closely in time and space. Like much child rearing theory (however did we raise children before so many theories?), this one works better on paper than on kids.

First, it applies better to toddlers and preschoolers, whose immediate world we can fairly well monitor and control. But once children reach six or seven years old, much of what they try or do we don't discover until time has intervened. Kids would love it if we rigidly adhered to a "misbehavior and discipline go together immediately or not at all" philosophy. As they get older they'd beat more and more raps because the ten-second statute of limitations ran out. They'd also get sneakier, as hiding misconduct even for just a little while would be greatly to their advantage.

If a child merits discipline, shouldn't he receive it? Teaching the lesson is primary; the timing is often secondary. Ideally, three-year-old Buford sits in a chair at Grandma's house for sassing Grandma. **Like much child rearing theory this one works better on paper than on kids.** If not possible for whatever reason, Grandma included, he sits at home at first opportunity, with a reminder of what he did. What matters is that there are consequences for mean talk, even if they come later than sooner.

Certainly good judgment is your guide. If the pens were pilfered two years ago, you may decide that talking about the incident will suffice. How often parents laugh with their adult children about the old days, saying, "Mom, remember how you never did find out who painted 'Mom, leave home' on the shed. Well, I have a confession to make. It was ... Sue."

The legal system applies a statute of limitations to most crimes. These are measured in years. Parents are generally more merciful than real life, but our true mercy comes from teaching lessons in love that last for years.

NINE

Reacting to Discipline: A Kid's Handbook

A ny discipline—no matter how kind, consistent, well-timed, or fair—runs headfirst into a central truth of parenting: Children don't like discipline. Certainly the better your discipline, the less overall resistance you'll face. But never, as long as kids are part of this parenting journey, will they completely cooperate in their socialization. That's why they need us.

The most common kid reaction to discipline—even worse misbehavior—we've covered from many angles in previous questions. We won't tread that ground again. Instead, we will respond to some other common kid responses to discipline. Having a good comeback to kid comebacks isn't just smart parenting. It will actually bring about better, or at least quieter, kid cooperation.

Don't Discipline Me; I Won't Like You

Dear Dr. Ray,

My daughter is four and has never been much of a discipline problem. Lately, though, she's begun saying, "I don't like you" when I do discipline her. I must admit I'm getting upset by it.

Unloved?

Of all the opinions kids hold about our discipline, "I don't like you" is among the first learned and most often said. It almost seems to roll off youngsters' tongues a few months after they've mastered "Momma" and "bye-bye." (I've often wondered whether there's any Freudian meaning to a child's learning "momma" and "bye-bye" at about the same time.)

A central truth of parenting is this: Kids do not see parenthood through the eyes of parents. Often what we do for their good makes absolutely no sense to them. They can't understand it, and they don't appreciate it. So they're very quick to let us know that they do not for one minute approve of it.

> A central truth of parenting is this: Kids do not see parenthood through the eyes of parents.

"I don't like you" (IDLY, for short) can also produce surges of guilt. What parent wants to be disliked by his or her children? Kids know this; they pick it up by osmosis somewhere between the ages of two and three. Little Lovina may just want to make you feel rotten about doing something that is in her best interests.

Despite her words, your daughter really does like you. Every day she sees that 95 percent of what's likeable in her life comes from you: love, security, praise—not to mention the true treasures—her Care Bear, the Disney Channel, and scratch 'n' sniff stickers. Even if she is downright displeased with you for the moment, she will get over it. Little kids react fast, but don't hold grudges. God bless them!

Don't you get upset with her sometimes, too, and not "like" her? That's nothing to be ashamed of; you're normal. You get over it, at least by bedtime, don't you? Don't you??

What can you do next time you hear an "I don't like _____?" (Fill in the blank with anything: "you," "this house," "Daddy," or as one precocious three-year-old said, "your brain.") The surest way to be instantly reliked would be to give Lovina exactly what she wants. Let her use your rare, two-day-a-year blooming violets as headpieces for the gerbil. In the short run, she'll be happy with you. In the long run, you'll most likely hear more unreasonable demands and more IDLY's.

One good way to respond to IDLY is idly. Let it pass. Even if it does sting some, it is only a fleeting burst of anger. Don't let it become a routine means of manipulating you or causing you undeserved guilt.

The first time I flung an IDLY at my mother, she smiled and said, "You're a little bit behind, Raymond. I stopped liking you two months ago." As young as I was, I heard what she was really saying: "That kind of talk won't keep me from doing what I'm doing."

There's a bright side to hearing "I don't like you." It can be one good sign you're teaching your youngster a valuable lesson. If you were liked all the time, you'd probably be parenting the way she thinks you should. And that's not good.

Laughing in the Face of Discipline

Dear Dr. Ray,

My daughter (age seven) sings or draws pictures with her fingers when I sit her in the corner. What do you do with a child who seems happy when she's disciplined?

Not Amused

What do you do? Nothing? Ask her if she takes requests? Threaten to remove her from the corner as punishment?

Just because Melody sings during discipline doesn't mean the discipline isn't working. It means that Melody is making the best of an inharmonious situation, and that's an admirable characteristic for anybody—child or adult—to cultivate.

I'm pretty sure your daughter doesn't enjoy the corner. If she did, periodically she'd mosey over there on her own just to sing and draw a few finger pictures. I'm also pretty sure that the only time she visits the

Parents routinely believe that for a consequence to work, kids have to be bothered or upset about it. Not so.

corner is at your request or command. If so, she's telling you something: the corner will be effective eventually. For now, though, she can get along with it if she has to.

Much to their frustration, parents routinely believe that for a consequence to work, kids have to be bothered or upset about it. Not so. By its very nature, discipline needs time—lots of it—to get its message across. Consequences typically have to be repeated dozens, if not hundreds, of times.

In your situation, the cumulative impact of the corner is what will make it work. For now your daughter enjoys herself in the corner. But that is certainly no cause for worry that she's unusual or that this is just the beginning of life with a child who will sabotage your every attempt to guide her.

A child's reaction to discipline generally is not a good indicator of whether you're on the right track. While Spike makes his discipline obvious to anyone within a three-mile radius, Bliss apathetically shrugs you off with a "give me your best shot—I don't care" style. In fact, apathy is a favorite kid reaction to discipline. Your daughter has just elevated apathy to a happier plane.

The best gauge of whether discipline will be successful is not a child's short-term attitude toward it, but her behavior in the long term. Let's say Harmony is singing her way through her tenth corner visit this week for her disrespectful tone of voice. (Try not to take it personally that she gets snotty to you but sings to the wall.) While she may still be amusing herself in the corner, away from it her mouth control is ever so slowly improving. And that's what counts.

A further consideration: Suppose you abandon the corner in search of something that will visibly upset Harmony, or at least stifle her singing. What's to say she won't make a good time out of the next consequence you try? Send her to her room, and she dances. Make her do an extra chore, and she plays house. Take away some TV, and she colors a great picture. I mean, the kid is just incorrigible.

If you just have to respond to Harmony, how about something like "You know, you really take your discipline well" or "I think it's wonderful how you can stay happy even when most people would get upset." The danger here, of course, is that she'll make a grand show of how happy discipline makes her just so you'll fawn all over her. Oh well, parenting often involves trade-offs.

I have one other question. Does Melody sing the same song or vary them? One mom told me her son whistled "It's a Small World" for weeks after they had visited Disney World. Now that would make me mad.

A Sorry State of Affairs

Dear Dr. Ray,

My seven-year-old son almost always says "I'm sorry" after he's done something wrong. He seems so genuinely remorseful that I'm not sure how to respond. As long as he's learned his lesson, do I need to discipline him, too?

Sorry Too

Let me begin by suggesting what you could *say* in response. How about, "Apology accepted," or "That's good to hear," or "I'm glad." What to *do* in response is the more important matter.

Most likely, one of two motives is guiding your son. One, he is truly sorry for what he did. He acted on impulse, or emotion, or temptation, and as the possibility of discipline draws near, he realizes more clearly what he did and regrets it.

Or two, he knows discipline is close by so he's learned that "I'm sorry" conveys a quick, "Mom, don't worry, my conscience has punished me so you don't have to." In essence, your son may be sorry he misbehaved, but he's really sorry he could be corrected for it.

> Your son may be sorry he misbehaved, but he's really sorry he could be corrected for it.

Which motive is it? It's hard to say. It could be a combination of both. It could change with the situation. For many kids, "I'm sorry" starts out pretty genuine, and then over time, if they see that it sometimes talks them out of trouble, "I'm sorry" slides more quickly off their tongue. A basic truth about kids: They learn real fast what works.

But whatever your son's reasons for "I'm sorry," they're not really relevant to your response. That is, whether he's remorseful or faking, you still must discipline misconduct.

Consider the adult world. If you stole a car, would the judge say, "OK, you really seem to regret what you did, so wax the car up, put a note of apology on the windshield for the owner, and we'll forget the whole thing"? Not too likely, unless your note is a really good one. There would be consequences. You did wrong, you were sorry, now you pay the price.

The fact that your son may be truly remorseful is only part of his lesson. The other part is that he must learn he will be held accountable for his conduct, not just by his feelings, but by his mother. True sorrow is a sign of developing conscience, but to keep his conscience developing, you have to discipline.

If your son says, "I said I'm sorry" as it becomes clear to him that you're following through anyway, he's giving himself away. He's telling you he's realized for some time now that "sorry" can be an escape word.

Then, too, sometimes little Justice may only apologize once discipline begins. Many a child's first words upon looking straight into the corner are "I'm sorry, Mom. I'll be good, forever." I mean, no sense wasting a perfectly good apology on only the risk of being in trouble. Wait until the trouble has actually begun, then feel pangs of conscience.

Is your son weaseling you? Maybe. Need you worry about his character if he is? No. Most kids are part weasel. That's normal. It's up to us parents to be part bulldog and train some of the weasel out of them.

I'm sorry if I upset you. Don't call my editor, OK? I really am sorry.

You Don't Love Me—Not!

Dear Dr. Ray,

What can I say to a seven-year-old girl who constantly says, "You don't love me"?

I Do Too

Nothing. That's my most succinct answer. But since my editors won't let me get away with that, let me go on.

First, a few basic assumptions. One, you're referring to your little girl and not some youngster you just met yesterday. Two, you do love your daughter and you show and tell her often. Three, this is her comeback when you are doing something loving, such as disciplining or setting rules and expectations.

Odds are all three assumptions are accurate, not because I'm so smart but because almost always each is present when loving parents are called unloving by a momentarily frustrated child.

"You don't love me" is pure nonsense. You know it and, believe it or not, so does your daughter.

Because this accusation is about as far from the truth as a child can get, it can really sting. If she said things like, "You always growl when I'm around" or "You like sleep better than me," we might in our more brutally honest moments silently admit to a few grains of truth there. But "You don't love me" is pure nonsense.

You know it and, believe it or not, so does your daughter. Temporarily she may think you don't love her because she's upset and her seven-year-old mind can't comprehend the long-range reasons for your actions. Or maybe she thinks no such thing but is hauling out her big guilt gun to shoot down your parental confidence.

How do kids know that this line hurts? At first, they can read our reaction, however subtle our flinch or pained look. Over time, they come to realize its power as we compulsively explain and reexplain ourselves each and every time they say it.

My hunch is that you repeatedly tell your daughter how what you're doing in no way whatsoever comes from a lack of love. (She reacts with disbelief.) In fact, if you didn't love her so much, you'd let her do anything she wants. (Incredible disbelief.) Finally, citing Parenting Manual Code 307.65-A, you tell her that you always love her but sometimes you don't like her behavior. (Gagging disbelief.)

These all make loving sense, but like most talk, they lose effect with too much repetition. Then begins the game of "I'll accuse you of something totally ridiculous and then you try to convince me how wrong I am and then I'll argue illogically and then you get frustrated and feel bad and then I win."

If you feel an overpowering urge to reassure, do so occasionally. To do it every time only leads to recycled frustration and unnecessary justification. Most of the time, a quiet "That's wrong" or "Yes, I do" or a silent head shaking "no" is plenty. And here we are, four hundred words later, back to my original advice: Say nothing, or little.

In previous chapters I've praised the wisdom of the stupid look. I think every parent needs to know how to look stupid on command and not just at random. The stupid look says: Not only will I not dignify that comment with a response, but

I don't even know what I'd say if I did respond.

I think it was a mother who observed: You never have to explain what you don't say.

Selective Hearing Loss

Dear Dr. Ray,

My oldest son constantly claims he didn't hear me after I've asked or told him to do something. There's nothing wrong with his hearing. I've had it tested.

Say It Again?

Sounds as though your son suffers from a widespread childhood affliction: Selective Hearing Loss (SHL). It plagues kids of all ages, typically becoming more acute in adolescence.

Contrary to popular belief, children don't always outgrow this disorder. Some become chronically afflicted as spouses. There is one main symptom: deafness to any words, particularly those of parents, that a youngster doesn't want to hear. Contrary to popular belief, children don't always outgrow this disorder. Some become chronically afflicted as spouses.

To determine if your son suffers from SHL, try this diagnostic test. Walk several blocks from your house, stand on the other side of an interstate highway or major thoroughfare, wait for a jumbo jet to pass overhead, and then whisper, "Forbes, would you like me to raise your allowance five dollars a week, and I'll make your sister do all your chores?" If he screams, "Sure!" the test is positive.

When your son claims SHL, one of two things is happening. In the first and more frequent instance, he did in fact hear you, but he's denying it to dodge your request or your wrath. Indeed, how can you blame him if the sound of the cat walking across the carpet drowned out your words?

In the second instance, he really didn't hear you, but this is because he has learned to tune you out. In either case, the treatment for SHL is the same, and it involves medicine taken in several steps.

Step #1. When you have something important to say, but suspect your son won't think likewise—whether it's as everyday as asking him to take out the trash or as weighty as reminding him about no house guest on Friday night because you'll be out late—say it with your mouth as close to his ear as possible. Resist the temptation to raise your voice. With kids, the softer you speak, the more impression you make.

This step may require a little extra walking on your part, but as long as there's a room, a wall, paper, or some air between you and your son, SHL is more likely to strike. A bonus of close-up speaking is that you're better able to pick up the slightest sign that Earhard did hear you, such as the hair standing up on the back of his neck.

Step #2. If possible, make eye contact. This isn't always easy, especially with kids whose eyes reflexively roll toward the ceiling at first sound of their parent's voice.

Step #3. Ask your son to repeat what you just said. Probably he'll semigrudgingly parrot back your words. That's OK, because here lies the ultimate cure for SHL. Now there is no way he can claim he didn't hear you. Of course, savvy kids can later fall back on "I forgot" (Juvenile Memory Deficit), but we'll treat this disorder in the next section.

As a maintenance treatment for SHL, hold your son accountable for his selectively poor hearing. If he didn't "hear" you tell him to come straight home after school, and consequently you require him to stay home tomorrow, his hearing acuity will improve with time. In other words, make sure he feels some consequence for not hearing.

One caution: Selective Hearing Loss is contagious. Not only can siblings catch it from siblings, but with prolonged exposure, even you might be afflicted. One mother told me that any time her kids approached her with, "Mom, will you ..." she blocked out the rest.

Juvenile Memory Deficit

Dear Dr. Ray,

My thirteen-year-old son seems to have a bad memory, but only where I'm concerned. If I ask, "Please take out the trash," a half hour later he says, "I forgot." If I ask, "Why aren't the dishes dried yet?" again I get, "I forgot." He only seems to forget what he doesn't want to do.

Easy to Forget?

Your son seems to have Juvenile Memory Deficit (JMD), which is the problem of forgetting unwanted words. To get some idea of how badly he suffers from JMD, try this diagnostic test. "Earhard, I promise I'll give you five dollars, one month from now. All you have to do to get it is to remember the exact place and time—to the second—that I made this promise. I'll ask you about it next month."

Some JMD kids actually have photographic memories, but only at select times. Kermit forgot to feed the turtle two minutes after being reminded for the third time, yet he can describe exactly how his brother didn't do what he was told to do on Friday morning at 7:10 three weeks ago. Even the worst case of JMD doesn't hamper a child's ability to remember your every transgression or "inequity" as a parent.

Once you've diagnosed JMD, you can apply the necessary medicine. The first dose is similar to that used for Selective Hearing Loss: Require your son to look you in the eye and repeat what you just said. While this is strong medicine for SHL—kids can't claim they didn't hear what they themselves said, or not legitimately, anyway—it is not foolproof for JMD. Faith can still claim she "forgot" what both you and she said.

Therefore, you may need more potent medicine. One experimental procedure has shown promise in clinical trials: Treat poor memory with poor memory.

For example, if your son forgets that three hours ago he was asked to take out the trash, you will forget what you asked. Was it to dry the dishes or take out the trash? Since you can't recall, he'll now do both, just to cover all the bases. If he has memory lapses—and he's young and healthy—how can he expect his mother, whose brain cells are part petrified, to remember everything?

At this point most kids instantly recall exactly what you

asked. (It's a miracle!) Nevertheless, it's too late. This time around there are added duties or consequences for ignoring Mom. As your son is held accountable for his forgetfulness, his memory skills should improve radically.

It's a psychological axiom that humans—little and big—often forget what they don't want to remember.

What if your son truly forgets? Sometimes he will. It's a psychological axiom that humans—little and big—often forget what they don't want to remember. Nevertheless, your intent is to teach your son to remember his responsibilities, whether he wants to or not.

It's possible that this section may never be read by anybody. You see, my editor gave me a deadline, and I don't recall when it was.

Just Trying to Cloud the Facts, Ma'am

Dear Dr. Ray,

Whenever my sons think they're in trouble, they start defending themselves with all kinds of excuses and "buts." They bring up every irrelevant point they can, it seems, just to out-argue me.

Word Weary

It's called quibbling. Most self-respecting kids have it mastered by age ten. Teenagers perfect the talent, able to quibble at an instant's notice. Neither is quibbling something to be hastily outgrown. When cornered, spouses, too, have been heard to quibble.

What exactly is quibbling? It is the art of muddling, side-tracking, and confusing. It is spewing verbal clutter and point-less nitpicking until the target (almost always a parent) collapses from exhaustion, thereby allowing the quibbler to escape responsibility for his or her actions. The quibbler's motto is "Keep 'em debating until the original issue is obliterated."

Quibble bouts are most likely to erupt anytime a youngster senses he is in imminent danger of being held accountable for his behavior. A scenario: Webb has wandered home an hour after school, clearly breaking the house rule of "Go nowhere after

> **Quibbling…is the art of spewing verbal clutter and pointless nitpicking until the target (almost always a parent) collapses from exhaustion.**

school without permission." Mom, with worry now turned to anger, asks what she believes to be a straightforward question, naively assuming she'll get a straightforward answer:

Mom: Where were you?

Webb (Quibble Rule #1: Never answer the question directly): I asked you last night if I could go over to Wendell's house for a half hour after school.

Mom: You asked, and I said, "I don't think so."

Webb: You said, "I don't think so. We'll see what the weather's like." Faith was there. She heard you. (A master quibbler cites ear witnesses, making sure they're unavailable during the actual quibble.)

Mom (getting outquibbled, tries a new tack): Even if you misunderstood me, you were gone an hour, not a half hour.

Webb: I was at Wendell's for only a half hour, helping his dad rake leaves (slick move, pointing out responsible behavior while facing charges of irresponsibility). Besides, it takes time to walk there from school and then home.

Mom: It takes ten minutes at most.

Webb: That's if I cut through people's yards, but I don't think it's right to do that. And I had to wait for both red lights, like you said I should. (This kid's a pro.)

Mom (weakening): Why didn't you at least call to tell me where you were?

Webb: I would have, but my feet were dirty and I didn't want to walk through Wendell's house. Plus, I lost track of the time because Wendell's dad talks so much.

This is merely the early phase of a quibble bout that will drag on as long as Mom partakes. Webb won't end it. Time is on his side. The longer it goes, the more chance he'll confuse Mom into feeling unfair if she disciplines him.

The only person to quell quibbling is you. The moment you suspect that this is occurring—typically within Webb's first or second comeback—identify the process: "We're quibbling. The real issue is that you didn't get permission to go anywhere after school. Because of that, you're grounded tomorrow night (or some similar price tag)." Then end the interchange.

One father dubbed quibbling "wordsmithing." Like verbal blacksmiths, his kids would bend, mold, and smash words and logic to fit their immediate purpose. Dad would ask, "Are you wordsmithing?" which meant, "Cease now, or you'll complicate your consequences."

Expect quibbling, or repeated attempts at it. With time, you'll get quicker at hearing what's happening and silencing it. Will your kids like your unwillingness to quibble? Of course not. They'll think you're being unfair, close-minded, stubborn, power-hungry, or any number of other adjectives that parents get accused of when we refuse to be pulled into childish interchanges.

Take comfort. In the long run you will be seen as kinder for not quibbling. Quibbling is arguing. And arguments generally don't make for good feelings on either side. Refuse to argue, and initially you may be misunderstood, but eventually you'll be better understood, and appreciated for it.

Apathy—Kids Work at It

Dear Dr. Ray,

Our ten-year-old son accepts discipline pretty well. In fact, he accepts it too well. Whenever I discipline him, I meet with an "I don't care." I'm frustrated by his total lack of reaction. What can I do if he really doesn't care?

I Care

Apathy—kids put a lot of effort into it. They deliberately work hard to convince you that discipline doesn't phase them. In other words, they care that you care that they don't care.

There are two basic parent-tested tactics kids use to convey apathy. Each sends a surge of frustration up parents' spines. Some kids will proclaim loud and clear, "I don't care," for example, upon hearing their phone privileges are disconnected until they pay off the phone bill listing 2,724 call-in votes (at fifty cents apiece) naming their favorite green-haired rock star.

Other kids elevate feigned indifference to its purest form. Barely giving you a listless shoulder shrug and mouth twist, Joy wants you to know she doesn't even care enough to tell you she doesn't care.

Most, if not all, "I don't care" messages are facade. If Nielson truly didn't mind losing TV until his room is clean enough to find the window, why would he spend time watching TV in the first place? If Penny genuinely wasn't bothered by paying you twenty-five cents for drying the dishes she "forgot" about, every so often, just out of gratitude that you're her mother, she'd walk up and hand you a quarter.

Kids care about discipline. They just don't want you to think they do, for two reasons. One, if you think that your twenty-five-cent penalty affected Penny, you just might try this fine approach more often in the future, and she certainly wouldn't want that. In any given year, she'd need to win the state lottery to pay you off. And two, Penny knows you're upset over her apathy, so at least she salvages something for her quarter.

On occasion, kids genuinely don't care about what you did. Carlisle's thinking, *So what if I can't have the car for a week. I don't need it*. But on his third car-less day, Carlisle gets a call from Carla, who says, "I have three free tickets to the Strawberry Asphalt concert, including a complimentary meal and autograph session with the band. Can you drive?" It took a few days, but Carlisle did find out that seemingly carefree consequences can lead to complications.

Too, always remember this discipline maxim: Your purpose is not solely to make kids care about your discipline. Your purpose is to place what you (or they) think is a fair consequence for their actions and then stick with it. Your goal is to teach Carlisle something about life, that is, that people are held accountable for their behavior, whether they care or not.

Kids who don't care do care, especially if we don't care that they don't care.

So what can you say or do in the face of apathy? Try meeting apathy with apathy. Don't say or do anything. Your calm will convey quite nicely that it doesn't matter to you that it doesn't matter to Joy. If you bounce all over looking for consequences that do seem to matter to her, you'll search endlessly, because Joy will most likely convey the same reaction regardless what you try. Kids stick with tactics that work on parents.

If you must say something, or you'll just burst, try, "I'm glad you're taking this so calmly." That usually takes the fire right out of apathy.

Apathy may be nerve-wracking, but it's simpler to handle than an argument or outright resistance. Kids who don't care do care, especially if we don't care that they don't care.

The Unfair Parent

Dear Dr. Ray,

If I hear "That's not fair" one more time from my son (age nine), I will scream. He throws it at me almost every time I discipline or expect him to do something his younger brother doesn't have to do.

Fairly Worn Out

Fair—the four letter word kids are most obsessed with. They expect—no, demand—that parents be 100 percent equitable, at all times, in all places, with all children. Even if we could accomplish this impossibility, we still would not get credit for it.

Kids define fair very personally. To young Justice, fair means getting disciplined equal to or less than his sister, Mercy, even though to be truly just, you would have to discipline him three times as much because he earns it. As it is, you let some misbehavior slide so as not to appear grossly biased.

"You're not fair" comes in limitless guises: "You like Robin better because she's your pet." "I'm nothing but a laborer around here." "How come you never send Jolie to her room?" "I'm going to treat my kids a lot better than you treat me."

If Holmes always considered you fair, that would be a sure sign you're not.

All such commentary on your parenting wraps around one theme: You simply are not acting with equity, as seen through juvenile eyes. Indeed, I hope not. Children are not exactly impartial judges of what is correct conduct, particularly where they're involved. Put another way, if Holmes always considered you fair, that would be a sure sign you're not.

Loving parents strive to be fair. You work at meting out time, attention, even material goodies in roughly comparable amounts. But because no two children are identical—even identical twins—no two parenting tracks are identical.

Butkus cleans his room anytime the sun comes up. Hazel won't touch hers unless you threaten to ground her until she owns her own home. Because of their distinct temperaments and personalities, children require very different approaches. They don't recognize this, so they sometimes interpret your legitimately dissimilar treatment of them as playing favorites or changing the rules in the middle of the game.

Another reality breeds the inequity charge: age. "Why do I have to go to bed now when Eve (older sister) gets to stay up later?" "When I don't pick up my toys, I lose them for a week. Murdock (four years younger) only loses his for three days."

Childhood is defined by ever-changing privileges and responsibilities. Ten-year-old Wendell enjoys greater freedom than his six-year-old sister. That's as it should be, he says. But at the same time, he chafes under your increased expectations. Neither Wendell nor his sister sees the whole picture. If they did, you wouldn't get nearly the complaints.

How can you mute the unfairness accusation? You'll never completely silence it. Even adults are quick to cry foul when we don't feel life is treating us fair. My first suggestion is to stop explaining yourself each and every time you hear "That's not fair." I'm sure you've plowed the same turf more than a fair number of times. In trying to talk a child into a grown-up's view of justice, the more you explain, the behinder you get.

A standard parental comeback is "Life's not fair." This is true, but kids don't buy it. At the moment of discipline, it's wise to live by another truth: The less said, the better. Explanations, if needed, are best reserved for later.

As your son gets older, you might consider something like this: "Justice, you really seem to be focused on having everything perfectly fair. So, from now on, when you complain, you'll write a two-hundred-word essay on fairness. This will help you better understand what you're talking about."

Don't despair. With time your son will realize that all is not fair and never will be. In fact, he'll see that parents are more fair than most people.

Parent Comparing

Dear Dr. Ray,

Am I the only parent who is tired of hearing my teenagers tell me how out of step I am with every other mother and father?

Measuring Up?

If you are, then you are the only parent in the world with teenagers. Parent-comparing may be adolescents' most time-tested way to make parents question themselves. I can almost hear fifteen-year-old George Washington, "But, Pop, Benny Franklin is allowed to prune his dad's cherry trees; you just don't trust me."

Kids draw comparisons for one basic purpose: to make you second-guess your decisions and change your mind—in their favor. Their goal is to convince you that you are not the in-touch parent that Lucky's mom is, and you're supposed to feel appropriately bad about that.

What self-respecting parent hasn't heard the likes of these comments: "Carson's mother lets him stay up until midnight." "Ebenezer's father doesn't make him spend his hard-earned allowance on school supplies."

Of course, no comparison is ever risked if it draws attention to anybody who has it "worse," for example, Madge, who helps her mother all morning Saturday with housework, or Oxford, whose dad makes him finish all homework before the TV goes on. Never! Heaven forbid that you should ever believe there are parents in this world stricter than you.

Seasoned parents are not without comebacks to parent comparing. Like these: "Well, you're not Carson." "We don't run our house the way Ebenezer's parents run theirs." Or the classic: "If Marlin jumps in the lake, will you jump in, too?"

> **If you really want to make Wiley pause, ask him, "How many nights a week is the average kid in Panama allowed to date?"**

No doubt you've tried these, and no doubt they had little, if any, impact, other than to make the kids mad. Why? Because teens don't want to hear this kind of logic.

Why? Because they're teens, and they think they have a pretty good idea of how they should be raised. And you are ignoring the crowd, which they aren't in the habit of doing.

So what can you do? First, brace yourself for comparisons. Expect that your decisions will be measured against dozens (thousands?) of other parents'.

In no way does this mean that you're a bad parent or even that your kids actually think you're below the national average. It has always amazed me how at any given moment the typical teen is aware of what *every* other kid in the Western Hemisphere is and isn't allowed to do. If you really want to make Wiley pause, ask him, "How many nights a week is the average kid in Panama allowed to date?"

Second, if you do rely on the standard comebacks, you'd probably do better to say them quietly, matter-of-factly, and *once*. Then let the subject drop.

You could show gratitude for the comparison. A genuine "thank you" will convey quite nicely that you are well aware of your individuality as a parent. Indeed, aren't your decisions based upon your values and your situation? Be thankful that your teen, however unwittingly, recognizes this.

In the end, your best response to a frivolous comparison may be silence. You don't need to debate your parental judgment versus Sherlock's mom. A blank look can wordlessly say that what others choose to do has absolutely no relevance to your parenting.

There's a bright side to being compared. In parenthood, the majority doesn't always provide a good example. If you're not like most moms and dads, it could be that your standards are a few notches above average. Feel proud.

After All I've Been For You

Dear Dr. Ray,

My son, age sixteen, often resists my rules with an attitude that says, "You say I'm a good kid, but it doesn't get me anywhere. I still don't have the freedom my friends have, and they give their parents a lot more trouble than I give you."

Ungrateful

Pick one:

    A. After all I've done for you, Mother, this is the thanks I get.

    B. You should be grateful I'm not as bad as all those other kids.

    C. What do you want from me? I'm not on drugs.

D. All the chances I've had to do bad things, and I haven't done them. You could at least ease up on me.

All of the above are variants of a common adolescent theme: "I'm playing by the rules, and you're still not willing to relax

I won't relax my standards simply because you've kept them. That's not good for you.

the rules." Let's analyze your son's attitude piece by piece.

"You say I'm a good kid, but it doesn't get me anywhere." Of course it does. It gets you good character, morals, and a more safe and stable adolescence. If the prime goal of being a good kid is to get more freedom, more perks, and more goodies, then you're not yet being good for the right reasons. Besides, why give you more chances to make bad decisions and maybe lose some of that goodness?

"I still don't have the freedom my friends have." That is true. If I wanted my son to do and have what most kids have, I'd raise him that way. No matter how wonderful you are, my decisions are based upon your continuing welfare. I won't relax my standards simply because you've kept them. That's not good for you.

"They give their parents a lot more trouble than I give you." I can't know that for sure, but I'll take your word for it. And that just proves my point.

You are who you are in part because we are who we are as parents. Therefore, why would I want to change the very ways that helped me raise a son like you? I'm proud of you, and I want to stay that way.

Your character is not measured by how you stack up to others with less character. It's measured by how you yourself act, independent of your friends' actions.

Your son is echoing a modern attitude. Coming from teens, it's the "I'm not on drugs" claim. Across all ages, it's "Well, I could be a lot worse. At least I'm not as bad as that guy." As cultural morals decline, it becomes easier to feel self-satisfied that one is comparatively moral.

Continue in your high standards, and your son will most likely mature past his moral relativity and judge character by more absolute standards of right and wrong. After all, he is still a kid, and a pretty good one. He has time to become morally more clear-eyed.

A final thought: Next time your son implies "You should be grateful," respond with, "You're right, I am grateful. It could be a lot worse. After all, I don't neglect you or mistreat you. And I'm not on drugs."

TEN

Disciplining Against the Flow

What kind of grown child do you want looking back at you at age twenty-two? The answer to this question determines the kind of parent you will be now.

If you wish to be able to say something like "I'm not real objective, I know, but that child is one in a thousand. Morals, character, maturity—a beautiful human being," then you must be prepared to be a one-in-a-thousand parent. Your standards will be different from, and higher than, the parenting norm. Thus you will be questioned, misunderstood, accused—not just by your children, that's to be expected—but by other adults: your friends, family, colleagues, experts. Indeed, it is a hazard of strong parenting today to be viewed as too strict, too controlling, too protective, too whatever, when in fact you are doing what is right and good by your children.

Stand strong. The wisdom of your ways will be evident for all to see in the quality of the people you're raising.

Good Grief

Dear Dr. Ray,

It seems that I get a lot of resistance, especially from friends and relatives, when I discipline my children. I'm no taskmaster, but I do want well-behaved children.

The Target

265

Picture the scenario. You're out somewhere, and someone hands your four-year-old a cookie. Now you've been working on manners since she toddled, so you're anxious for some parental payoff. Indeed, manners make parents look very good in public. That's why kids don't use them.

Without a word, little Grace begins to chomp. So you help her out: "What do you say?" More chewing, no words. "What are the magic words?" Dumb look, as if to say, what exactly is your point?

Being a veteran parent, you try a nonverbal approach. Taking your thumb and index finger, you reach behind her elbow, squeeze, and, gritting your teeth, quietly urge in her ear, "Say thank you." At last she talks: "Owww, you're hurting me!"

In a fit of parental resolve you take the half-chewed cookie, hand it back to the giver, explaining, "Thank you, but we have a rule. She knows she needs to say 'thank you,' or she can't keep it. And I prompted her three times just to avoid a scene."

Does the giver gape at you, astonished, and exclaim, "Good for you! You know, you don't see parents standing their ground like they should these days." Then turning to your daughter, she says: "Honey, you are very fortunate to have a mom who does this. You don't like it now, but you will when you're grown up."

Not in the real world. Instead, you're much more likely to hear something akin to "Oh, that's all right. In fact, here you go, little one, I have three more bags for you because you live with the *Wicked Witch of the West!*"

Keep in mind that this is just about teaching manners. It's not about the big stuff: morals, character, peers, academics, dating. This is just manners. So why are you getting grief for this? Simple. You have a standard, and you're enforcing it.

A paradoxical mind-set has infected our culture. People still want well-behaved and delightful children, and they bemoan that fewer and fewer seem so. Yet they resist and challenge the very things you need to do to raise such children. Parents who set the character bar high and discipline accordingly are more and more being met with questions, comments, doubts, and sometimes outright interference from surrounding adults.

> **The irony is that, after a decade or more of standing strong against all sorts of cultural commentary on their "strict" parenting, good parents are often rewarded with "You have great kids" by those most critical of their parenting over the years.**

The irony is that, after a decade or more of standing strong against all sorts of cultural commentary on their "strict" parenting, good parents are often rewarded with "You have great kids" by those most critical of their parenting over the years. One mom told me she had to fight the temptation to respond with "Well, which is it? Do I have great kids, or was I an Attila the She-Witch for all those years? It can't be both."

I'm not speaking here of parents who are nasty, arbitrary, and dictatorially controlling. I'm speaking of loving moms and dads with high, healthy standards. Such parents are getting less resistance from their children than from the very people who should know better, and who, as a general rule in our society a couple of generations ago, did know better: other adults.

I fear the parenting continuum has shifted markedly

toward the permissive in the past thirty years. As a result, those who would have once been considered typical in their attitudes and practices are now variously seen as really tough, overly strict, rigid, or too controlling. In fact, they're nothing of the sort. But relative to the crowd, they look unusual or extreme.

By their fruits you will know them. The proof of great parenting will show clearly in the children. The grief you're getting is good grief. It's a sign, I believe, that you're doing what is right for your children. It is ultimately your children who—as their character unfolds and they too become parents—will begin to shift the parenting continuum back to where it belongs.

Strictly Speaking

Dear Dr. Ray,
Can a parent be too strict?

Accused

Yes and no. (We shrink types are trained to make these kinds of definitive pronouncements.) Yes, a parent can be too strict, if strict means mean. No, she can't, if strict means high moral standards.

Commonly, strict is confused with volume, or strong emotions, or verbal barrage. Consider an argumentative adolescent. Think of the neighbor kid if you have to. As the dueling interchange begins, we begin:

"Young man, are you arguing?"

"No," followed by more arguing.

"That is just about enough!" Not really, as more than enough continues.

"I will not tolerate that tone of voice. You watch your mouth." Still more.

"That's it. This discussion is done with. Keep going and you won't drive until Social Security."

As the words escalate, so too do our tone and emotions. We appear to be standing strong. Yet we are doing nothing but arguing and being loud.

No consequences have been placed upon Buck's misconduct. No discipline has occurred. We may have looked, even sounded, tough. But in reality, we were weak and permissive.

> **Nowadays, strict has become a bad-sounding word. It conjures up all sorts of other bad-sounding words: rigid, unyielding, dictatorial.**

Nowadays, strict has become a bad-sounding word. It conjures up all sorts of other bad-sounding words: rigid, unyielding, dictatorial. In essence, it evokes a you'll-do-it-my-way-kid-because-I'm-the-boss style.

Of course, the parent *is* the boss, but that's not the prime motive for discipline. Forming morals and character is. Bossiness for bossiness' sake is too strict. Being the boss in order to teach is not too strict. It's ultimately kind.

Within a loving home, being too strict shouldn't be a worry, if strict means expecting good conduct. Indeed, what constitutes "expecting too much" in terms of moral goals? How high are standards that are too high?

Suppose you have a house rule: All family members show respect toward all family members. How do you ensure that you're not overly frustrating the kids with your rule?

"OK, children, you are each allowed three snotty outbursts, two name-callings, and one kick below the neck per day toward your siblings. Anything over that will be disciplined. We want to keep our standards realistic here."

If protecting little Nielsen from amoral television is a parenting priority, do you put up an impervious screen or a semi-porous one? Do you shield him from *all* nasty stuff, or do you allow one sexy sitcom, two brutal local news stories, and one afternoon talk show just to make sure he won't react too negatively to your decision, or won't feel like a misfit compared to his peers?

Raising a great kid requires setting the moral bar high, likely much higher than most parents around you. Certainly this doesn't mean your children will always, or even consistently, reach that bar. The most grown up of grown-ups don't clear the moral bar much of the time. Still we all need something to stretch for.

Rebelling Without a Cause

Dear Dr. Ray,

What do you think about the idea that if parents are "too strict" or put their moral standards too high, a child will ultimately just rebel?

Strict But Wavering

I think it is utter nonsense. How's that for psychologically sugarcoating my answer? Of all the parent-assaulting, authority-undercutting ideas that blanket the child rearing landscape today, this one gets my vote as ranking among the worst.

Certainly if parents are dictatorial and unloving, they risk raising a child who sees little rationale or warmth underlying the standards, and who may ignore or challenge those standards with time. As one expert puts it, "Rules without relationship can breed rebellion."

The critical difference between strong parenting *with* love and strong parenting *without* love, however, is often ignored. Implicitly, the warning is that, no matter how much love, if you expect too much good behavior or you are too different from the parenting crowd, you're asking for psychological trouble. Your high expectations will be the very thing leading to your child's unruliness. This notion finds a face in the stereotype of the "preacher's kid" who, as everyone knows, is the sneakiest, most morally profligate kid of the bunch.

As long as free will exists, there are no parenting guarantees.

Truth be told, most preacher's kids are more moral and mature than the norm. False notions are fueled by the exceptions that do fit the stereotype.

Some kids will rebel against good rules and limits, regardless of how loving their parents are. As long as free will exists, there are no parenting guarantees. But again, these are the exceptions, and of these, many only temporarily rebel before finally and fully embracing what they were taught for years.

The most crippling aspect of this nutty notion is that it

keeps parents from resolutely taking the stands that deep down they know are right for fear of somehow emotionally pushing their children away. After all, Dorothy already thinks she has the Wicked Witch of the West for a mother and Attila the Hun for a father. So, you'll only make things worse by being "too controlling" in your rules. You need to compromise your moral position here and there so as not to appear unreasonable.

It seems to me that once upon a time, back before the onslaught of all the experts and their theories, parents instinctively understood that it was healthy to set high standards and enforce them vigorously. This led to good kids, not rebellious kids. Now it seems that this instinct is being challenged.

Set your bar too high, the new wisdom says, and your children's resistance is a sure sign that you're being too pushy about this whole parenting thing. On the contrary, however, it's a sure sign that you're a parent and they are kids.

But what if you are clearly way above the parenting norm in your social supervision, in the chores you require, in the respect you expect, and so on? Won't your kids draw comparisons: "How can all those people be wrong and you be right?"

Sure they will. And they'll resist you even more than they otherwise would if more people thought as you do. Stand strong. The results you want—great kids—will happen, even if your ride is bumpy, and you are much misunderstood along the way.

Generating Generational Tension

Dear Dr. Ray,

What can I do about my parents who think I'm being too strict or too mean when I discipline my four-year-old daughter? The irony is that they were even more strict raising me.

What Happened?

As Bill Cosby says, "These are not the same people who raised us. These are older people now trying to get into heaven."

Asking my father for a nickel for a Popsicle when I was a kid involved submitting a comprehensive fiscal plan detailing how many days of chores I'd be willing to do to earn it, what size the Popsicle, what percentage of the nickel I'd give to the church, all negotiated through a federal arbitrator. Thirty-five years later, this is the same man who accuses me of depriving my children if I deny them a third helping of the five-pound bucket of ice cream he brought over. I don't know exactly what's happened, but I do know such a dramatic change is not uncommon.

What you can do about your folks' disagreement with your parenting depends upon their level of disagreement. If they just *think* you're too strict—although they must have voiced it at some time for you to know they think it—you don't have to do much. Continue raising your daughter as you see best, even in their presence, knowing they don't fully concur.

With time they'll see what a good kid you're raising, and

they'll conclude one of two things: One, you were right all along. Or two, your child is managing still to grow up fine despite having Cruella DeVille for a mother. Most conclude the first.

Level-two interference involves second-guessing out loud of your disciplining—in front of you or your daughter. Here, a first step is to speak up. "Mom, I know you don't always like how I raise Bliss, but you always taught me to do what I believe is right." Or "Dad, it really confuses Storm when she sees us disagree, and she's likely to act even worse."

If you want to be a little more forceful, you can say, "You raised me beautifully, Mom and Dad, so I'm going to do it just the way you always did it." The converse would be: "Well, you had your chance with me, and look what happened. So I'm making some changes." Of course, I would *never* recommend saying anything like this last, even if it's true.

Level-three interference is active, purposeful undercutting of your authority. You send Sybil to the corner, and your mom takes her out. You limit her donuts to one half, and your dad gives her half a dozen.

Two suggestions: One, if you can do it without ugly conflict, calmly override your parents. Simply make your discipline stick in the face of their resistance.

Two, create no dispute on the spot, but inform your daughter that if she listens to Grandma instead of Mommy, she'll face more trouble when Grandma or Grandpa is not around. In other words, her accepting Grandma's corner time pardon will lead to extra corner time at home, as well as loss of, say, dessert. It may take several months, but the average kid will learn to act in harmony with a parent instead of siding with Grandma or Grandpa, in order to avoid facing the music at home.

The most relationship-straining level of interference would involve your folks' deliberately being unwilling to respect your requests and standards when your daughter is alone with them. In essence, Disneyland without limits is the scene. Here, if all attempts to get cooperation have failed, you are forced into some tough decisions. You could bear with the low standards, confident you can undo them with your own higher standards at home.

The alternative is to limit the amount of one-on-one time Harmony spends with her grandparents. Certainly most parents don't want to have to take this course of action, but some cases are so extreme that nothing short of it will protect your right to raise your child with your goals and morals. I hope this is not your situation.

In fairness to grandparents everywhere, I must acknowledge that I hear often from grandparents something like "You know, I'd like to spoil my grandkids a bit, but their parents already let them get away with so much that I feel as if I have to be the disciplinarian."

Material Discomforts

Dear Dr. Ray,

I'm getting more and more uncomfortable with the amount of toys, gifts, and general "stuff" that my children receive. Well-meaning relatives and my husband and I have overdone it. The kids have gotten less appreciative and more bored.

Too Well-Off

You are asking two questions. One, how can you and your husband cut back on your excess? And two, what can you do to slow down the supply and resupply from loving relatives? Let's focus on you first. Then we'll talk about your relatives behind their back.

The first law of child rearing economics is this: Don't give materially all you are able to. The second law is like unto it: Don't give materially all a child wants you to. Many rationales push parents into breaking these laws. Here are common ones.

1. I want to give my children what I didn't have.
2. I like to see them happy and excited.
3. So many other families' kids have it.
4. We can afford it.

Let's consider these individually.

1. *I want to give my children what I didn't have.* If this means love, attention, time, affection, praise, then by all means flood them with it. It's hard to give too much of these good things. They are gifts that can't be broken, hoarded, or fought over—well, most of the time. (Sometimes the worst brawl can erupt over who gets to sit on Dad's lap first.)

Certainly you want to give your kids a higher standard of living, but going too far may lower their level of living.

If your childhood was materially poor, certainly you want to give your kids a higher standard of living, but going too far may lower their level of living. Materialism can be a forerunner to self-centeredness, endless demands, ingratitude, boredom. I have seen few children lacking for character because they lacked for material perks. I have seen quite a few who lacked for it because they were indulged.

2. *I like to see them happy and excited.* In the short term, lots of gifts excite kids. But humans are creatures of habituation. We grow accustomed to things, and what was once exhilarating loses luster.

Consider your son's glee upon opening his first gift on Christmas morning. He wants to linger and play. But there is a whole stack yet to consume. By gift number seven, he's in full ripping frenzy, stopping only long enough to reach for the next surprise. Another human trait: The more we get, especially if it's free, the less we appreciate it. And we often come to expect it.

3. *So many other families' kids have it.* The pressure from this perception is most acute concerning the latest games, gimmicks, clothes, and ninety-dollar athletic shoes. Whether or not 999 homes of 1,000 sport the latest designer lunch-box is completely irrelevant to whether your home should have it. Good parenting is not majority parenting. You can be different. Maybe your parenting is better than most.

Will your youngster feel cheated or apart from the crowd? Possibly, in this small matter. But whatever tiny, temporary identity issue this might cause will be more than offset by the lesson he's learning about life, himself, and moderation.

4. *We can afford it.* I won't dally on this one but will instead refer you back to the first law of childrearing economics. The fact that buying for your children puts little strain on your wallet bears no relationship whatsoever to what's good for your child. Certainly you can also afford many harmful things, but you would never consider getting them. In themselves toys and goodies aren't trouble, but in excess quantity they can breed qualities that are.

Good parenthood evolves. It's a long process of scrutinizing, rethinking, and changing—if need be—ideas that aren't working out well. All parents follow some notions that eventually show themselves to be faulty. Materialism is a common one. You're a wise parent. You've realized that even the best of intentions can teach unintentional lessons.

Next we need to recognize the corollary to the two laws of child rearing economics we have noted: Where your child is concerned, others need to follow your laws.

So how do you cap a bottomless well of material—from within your home and without? Here are three suggestions:

1. Gently seek your relatives' cooperation with your revamped mind-set. "We're going to cut way down on the things we buy the kids. We want to teach them more about appreciation. Can you help us? We know how much you enjoy getting them things, but we want them to love you for you and not what you can buy." Stress how much more their presence means than their presents.

2. If goodies continue to flow into the house at an unacceptable rate, you might begin an all-out campaign to reduce inventory. Together, you and the kids decide what to share with other children who have much less. Arrange for their personal delivery—to a hospital, shelter, group home, school, or church.

To avoid future accumulation, how about this rule: For every goodie that comes in, one goes out. The kids can choose. If they're reluctant to part with anything, you can choose.

Also, you might quietly tell Hughes that he can't keep everything he gets from everybody. In your judgment, it's too much. This means some things may be given away almost as quickly as they arrive.

Is this being ungrateful or insulting to the givers? If they know what you're doing—of course, the kids will tell them—initially they might take it that way. But with time they should come to accept, if not understand, your "eccentric" ways. Your children's character is far too important for compromise on contributions you don't agree with, no matter how well intentioned the contributor.

3. Christmas has become a season of material excess, for children and adults. To regain some control of the spigot, prior to the holidays, you and the kids can sift through existing toys, deciding which will be given to other, more needy children. Make sure a few good items are shared, and not just the five-year-old, outgrown, untouched clutter.

Space out Christmas gift opening, so Noel can savor the gift and appreciate the giver. If too much flows in, hold over some for opening after Christmas.

You can make an even stronger statement about sharing by having the kids choose one or two unopened gifts to be given to a less-fortunate child. Because the package contents are unknown, a child will truly be sharing and not just discarding the least favorite gift.

Will relatives and friends understand? Again, maybe not. But they probably will be amazed by your resolve actively to teach what you preach.

Do you have the right to give away gifts? Of course. Once given, a gift is the receiver's to do with what he or she wishes, even to regive to another.

But aren't you "taking" your children's gifts? Yes and no. Yes, in that you may initially be doing these things against their will. No, in that you are acting in their long-term interests, and as a parent, you have that responsibility.

Indeed, you use your influence and authority to direct your children's actions all the time. You take the fourth cookie Chip tries to eat. You take Neilsen's remote control after an hour of TV viewing. You take Locke's freedom by sending him to his room. Not allowing access to bad things, or to good things in bad quantity, is a form of loving parenting.

Isn't all this just "forcing" kids to share or to be less materialistic? Sure it is. Much of character is instilled initially by making kids do or not do things against their wishes.

At first most kids do resist giving up what is "theirs" or are upset about not getting more. As they mature, however, they begin to grasp the deeper reason behind the action. They feel better about giving than getting, and learn to be content and grateful for what they have rather than upset over what they don't have.

If kids naturally refused excess, you wouldn't have asked the questions you did.

A Stream of Stuff

Dear Dr. Ray,

My kids are ages seven and four. It seems everywhere we go somebody is giving them something—candy, a toy, a trinket of some kind. They're coming to expect it.

Treats R Us

Someday I'm going to design a study. I'll randomly select a child to receive at least one free material goodie per day from wherever. It shouldn't be too hard to arrange. Nowadays kids get a plastic ring for getting their hair cut, a sucker for getting their ears examined, gum for memorizing a

> With a little hoarding and planning, the average kid can have his own yard sale about once a month.

Bible verse in CCD, and a Mickey Mouse eraser for turning in three reading papers at school. Indeed, with a little hoarding and planning, the average kid can have his own yard sale about once a month.

Next, I'll take my study measurements. How many days will it take before my subject asks for a treat from someone who didn't give one? Or gets upset if he doesn't get one? Or says, "I don't like that. I've already got one of those"? I suspect the results will depend upon how much was received how often and from where.

This is not to speak ill of children. It's more a comment on human habit. It doesn't take people long, especially the younger ones, to see constant freebees as entitlements. Therefore, I'm going to conclude your sons are human. (Years of training helps me make such deep insights.)

How can you reverse this process that is teaching your sons something you don't want them to learn? Well, there's good news and there's bad news. The good news: You're the parent. Quit allowing everyone to trinketize them.

Simply screen out some of it. Here and there, of course, material perks are fun and benign. It's the relentless cumulative effect you need to resist.

The bad news? People won't let you be the parent so easily. Certainly they can't see any problem in giving Rich a rubber spider. It's a small display of affection. It's a good thing. What they don't know is that it's the seventeenth goodie he's gotten this week, and it's not bringing out good things in him. To get a feel for the resistance you'll meet, do your own study.

Next time you're at a fast-food restaurant and your children order a kid's meal, tell the clerk, "That's OK, you can keep the toy." Initially, you'll receive a sympathetic look of bewilderment.

"No, ma'am, you don't understand. You see, on our planet, the toy comes with the meal. It's free. Did you want some extras?"

So, you explain yourself further. "No, please, keep the toy. I think it's privilege enough that I'm taking them out to eat. They don't need a toy too."

Besides, you know what happens at home. You step on this junk for three weeks, finally sneak it into the trash at two o'clock in the morning, dump coffee grounds on top of it, only to hear the next morning, "Hey, how'd that get in there? I only got sixteen of those, and that was my favorite one."

After your second explanation, the clerk's look of sympathy will probably turn to stunned disbelief, as if to imply, "You call yourself a mother." Before you leave, ask one more question. "Have you ever had anyone do this before?"

I can almost guarantee the answer: "No, you're the first." Of the tens of thousands of parents who have ordered those toy meals, you're the first weirdo actually to refuse the toy. Does that make it clear how you will be perceived for taking a reduced goodies stand?

A final consolation to shore you up. Though some, including your kids, will see you as a radical, over-the-edge parent, you will be imparting a truly valuable gift to your children: the gift of real gratitude for what they do receive. And who knows, maybe someday their spouses will thank you profusely.

Friendly Persuasion

Dear Dr. Ray,

My sons are ages eight and eleven. I know I can't pick their friends, but I worry about who they choose.

A Picky Mother

Who says you can't pick their friends? Somewhat anyway. Would you allow your eleven-year-old to watch an R-rated movie? How about the basic afternoon TV talk show fare? Would you let him leaf through an "adult" magazine? Can he take in a birthday party with no adult supervision?

Most likely your answers are no, no, no, and no. Why? Because you know that one of your prime parental duties is to protect, to shield your children from risk and harm, both physical and emotional. And the younger the child, the wider your sphere of protection must be. Young children have neither the moral base nor maturity to make consistently wise decisions about life.

If you're like most parents, you are more confident monitoring impersonal influences—media, movies, video games. Decisions get more fuzzy when the influence is personal, that is, another child. Unfortunately, other kids can carry a lot of unwanted worldliness to your children.

Any child whose innocence is fast eroding, through association, may wash away some of your son's still childlike innocence.

Where character formation and peer relations clash, choose in favor of character.

My belief is that it's every bit as important to distance your children from worldly people (however young) as it is from worldly things. Where character formation and peer relations clash, choose in favor of character.

Ultimately, all situations require your judgment, because other kids are far more complex an influence than video games. For example, the neighbor boy, Ash, may possess and be proficient in every known flammable device. Obviously, you wouldn't want him within a flare's distance of your house.

On the other hand, Duke is not into arson or burglary, but his vocabulary can be salty and he thinks rules are for wimps like your son. Still, overall he adheres to your rules.

One option is to allow your sons to play with Duke sparingly and only at your place. Keep a close ear on happenings (do you have security cameras?), and clearly tell Duke and your sons that if anyone says or does what you don't permit, Duke is gone for x time and your sons are inside.

There is a bonus in such vigilance. You're probably too stifling for Duke. He'll either force himself up to your standards, or he'll tire of you and your sons.

No matter what you do, your boys will have some contact with kids growing up way too fast. Our popular culture is breeding lost childhoods. Even if you closely monitor the home front, there are still plenty of other places to see and hear too much too soon.

Your goal is to shield your sons fully for as long as you judge wise, and to minimize those times and places when and where they are surrounded by others with fewer standards. As they mature, they will be better able morally to fend for themselves. Bad influences will be less influence because your parenting has been the strongest influence.

Old Young

Dear Dr. Ray,

My twelve-year-old thinks she's fifteen. She wants a lot more freedom than I think is good for her age. How can I convince her she's not fifteen?

Aging Fast

You can't. Not with words anyway. Once kids start creeping toward double-digit ages, they increasingly think they should be treated older than their age—in freedoms and rights, not in duties or responsibilities, of course. What ten-year-old says, "Gee, Mom, I think I'm old enough to buy my own clothes and do my own laundry."

The issue is not that your daughter wants more than you're willing to give her. Almost all kids want more than is good for them. And growing up is a push-and-pull negotiation with parents over how much we'll give them when. The real issue is how do you teach your daughter that, to the best of your ability, you will not allow her to grow up faster than her years.

> **The world offers them freedoms at ages when their counterparts of just a generation or two ago were still content to be kids.**

A good bit of your daughter's desire to be fifteen is driven by our society. Children are immersed in a popular culture that strips them while still young of their innocence. The world all around them relentlessly tempts and tells them to be discontent with who they are and what they have. It offers them freedoms at ages when their counterparts of just a generation or two ago were still content to be kids. Consequently, you are forced into vigilance, into resisting that culture for your daughter's sake, as you strive to give her a few more years of worry-free childhood.

I emphasize this to help you realize that what has always been natural to kids—pursuing more liberty than parents are willing to give—has been dramatically intensified by our society. You still can win. But it now takes far more effort to protect, supervise, and say no.

So, how do you keep a twelve-year-old a twelve-year-old? By treating her like a twelve-year-old. By giving and allowing her only what you judge is good for her, no matter what she thinks. Your question—"How can I convince her she's not fifteen?"—has two answers. You can't and you can.

You can't in the sense that she will seldom agree with your "stifling" parental decisions. She's a child, and children are notorious for not seeing the world our way. But you can in the sense that you will essentially force your daughter to live as a twelve-year-old. With time she will most likely better accept her lot in life—as a child with child freedoms, child privileges, and child responsibilities.

Even the most stubborn reality resisters (a.k.a. children) eventually quit kicking and screaming against the wisdom of their parents. Some take months, some take years, and most become parents themselves.

Doesn't it seem as if this is just one more example of how life is wired backwards? Children spend years wanting to be more grown up than they are—only to be grown up one day and nostalgically long only for the simplicity and innocence of youth.

TV or Not TV

Dear Dr. Ray,

I think our children (ages twelve and fourteen) watch too much TV. When we try to limit them, they feel deprived socially that they can't discuss all the popular shows with their peers. Do kids need television to interact with their peers?

Remote-Controlled

Kids don't *need* television for anything. They may want it, crave it, even suffer withdrawal during a power outage, but healthy social development is not linked remotely to the number of channels your set receives. If it were, installing a state-of-the-art satellite dish would make your kids overachievers.

Television is not inherently bad. Unlimited and un-screened, however, it is destructive. It erodes family life, promotes passive existence, and relentlessly beams distorted reality and morals at children. The key to making the medium work with your parenting rather than against it lies in how wisely it is controlled and dispensed.

Awareness of what's coming into your living room is critical to responsible TV guiding. Filtering out graphic violence or inappropriate sexual content is basic. But don't stop there.

Many parents confess that when they finally watched what their children were routinely watching, they sat stunned.

Even seemingly benign sitcoms and cartoons may contain themes and messages that run completely counter to your values. Many parents confess to me that when they finally watched what their children were routinely watching, they sat stunned. They had no inkling of the amount of junk food in their kids' video diet.

Even closely screened television is best limited. Otherwise, it can encroach upon a more well-rounded family existence. Here are some possible ground rules.

1. Television is available only after homework and chores are complete. Responsibilities preempt privileges.

2. No television on school nights. This ruling evokes comebacks from kids like these: "There's not another kid in the whole school whose parents do this. What am I going to talk about on the bus?" He may be right. That's irrelevant. How your family views television is your decision.

3. Programming can be rationed. Commercial stations are limited to half an hour per night. Public television can be watched up to an hour and a half.

4. Pay TV is now in place. Each half hour costs, say, ten cents. A PBS half hour costs a nickel, not because it's worth less, but because it's usually worth more. The money can be accumulated to help pay for a family outing.

One mother told me of an unexpected advantage of closely monitoring her kids' television, especially on Saturday mornings. They asked for fewer toys because they weren't nearly so aware of what to ask for.

A Room With a View

Dear Dr. Ray,
Do you think a teenager should have a television in his room?
Spouses Who Disagree

No. In print, my response to your question looks quiet and calm. If you could hear my answer, it would sound something like *No-o-o-o!!!*

A mother once told me that her fourteen-year-old son was given a television by his grandmother. Mom abhorred the idea of a TV in her son's bedroom, mostly because of its moral—or lack thereof—content, but Grandma warned, "I gave it to him. It is now his, and if you take it out, you'll deal with me." In an effort to sustain a shaky peace, Mom had acquiesced.

She asked me if I thought she had the right to take something someone had given her son. I asked, "If a classmate gave your son a bag of marijuana, would you confiscate it?"

"Of course," she said.

"Why?"

"Because it is harmful to him."

I replied, "Then you've answered your own question. You not only have the right, but the duty, to protect your son from harmful influences, from wherever they come." The fact that it was Grandma causing the problem complicated the family picture, but she had boxed Mom into a corner with her gift's conditions, effectively forcing her to choose between her son and family strife.

Grandma's attitude was "What does this harm?" Sadly, so often in modern parenting that is the guiding question. And if a parent can't provide a compelling "harm," her stand may crumble, and she'll find herself yielding to the opinions of others, her children's desires, or the flow of the culture's winds. If you view parenting as the imparting of morals and character to children over the course of twenty or so years (in some cases, over the course of thirty or more), *the*

The question is not, "What does this harm?" but rather "What good does it impart?"

question is not, "What does this harm?" but rather "What good does it impart?"

Using the latter question, though we could also use the former to provide plenty of reasons to unplug your son's personal TV, let's make our case.

In the area of morals, is standard TV fare in line with your values? Will it reinforce all you're trying to teach? Will it uplift your son's mind and spirit? Do the attitudes it promotes— toward faith, parents, authority, self-restraint, sex, family—fit well within your own?

If you've answered "yes" to these questions, then at least from a character perspective, television is your ally. Its unsupervised presence in your son's room will help to complete any areas of moral development your parenting may have missed.

Let's consider family time. Will the television nudge your son closer to the family or pull him from it? If you're not sure, answer this question: Is TV more entertaining than you are?

Kids are naturally attracted to being entertained. Will your relationship with your son deepen because of TV's vying for his attention? Will your son seek refuge more, or less, in his room if the television is there? Will the amount of family time increase or decrease if you're competing with thirty-seven channels and a remote?

Some parents qualify their TV placement with "It doesn't have cable, and the reception isn't real good." I've often wondered if this was their best defense or their only.

How about activity? Does the availability of private viewing raise or lower the likelihood your son will read, do schoolwork, interact with siblings, do chores, lift weights, even converse with you? Will the room television option broaden your son's horizons or narrow them?

In making wise decisions regarding our children's welfare, many questions often must be answered. And the answers may not lead us where much of society is headed. But they will serve to clarify just what may be the results of a particular decision. There is no doubt in my mind that our fast-forward culture is making parenting an emotionally turbulent ride. Why allow things into your family that only will work against what you are working for?

Good by Comparison

Dear Dr. Ray,

I have long been upset over the chronic condition of my fourteen-year-old's room. When my friend saw it, she laughed and said that I'm overreacting—I should see her son's room.

Calm Down and Lighten Up?

Why should you see her son's room? In your eyes, your son's room is plenty gross enough. In an earlier chapter we already addressed the issue of how to get a clean room, but we should still analyze your friend's comments on several levels.

Level one: She says her son's room is less habitable than your son's. All that really tells us is that there are two rooms in your homes in a similar trashed state. While her son's may be objectively worse than yours, she is less displeased by it.

That's her prerogative as a parent. But it is irrelevant to

whether or not your son's room should be acceptable to you. Your room standards may very well be different.

Level two: Should it give you solace that there are kids more sloppy than yours? Any parent can always find children more frustrating, defiant, rude, irresponsible, ungrateful, or whatever than their own. So? All that says is that the harder you work to raise good human beings, the less other people will be like you.

There is no comfort in comparing favorably to others if their standards are set lower. That's easy to do. The question is this: How do you compare to your own standards?

Level three: Your friend is implying that your son is normal for his age, at least where rooms are concerned. That's true. The majority of teenage boys have rooms that would be condemned by local building codes.

On the one hand, that's good to know. It can keep you from reading too much into certain behavior. It is soothing to know that what Butler is doing is not atypical, bizarre, or pathological. That can keep you from overreacting, as your friend says.

On the other hand, just because your son's conduct is normal doesn't mean it's good or desirable. What are acceptable room conditions among young boys may not be acceptable among mothers, who just happen to own the house that is built around the room. You have every right, even the responsibility, to set your standards where you wish, not just for your sake, but for your son's. You will teach him to cooperate with legitimate authority even when he does not agree with it. And that's a virtue that's getting less and less normal in our culture.

Level four: You need to relax and accept your son's room as

is because he's not doing anything that bad, says your friend. Yes, in the overall scheme of parenting, disheveled rooms are down on most parents' priority lists. But again, in no way does this mean you have to accept the room.

If all the other parents jump into the lake, are you going to jump in, too?

Maybe your friend was implying that you are getting too upset over this issue. That's possible—in which case, you can tone down your words, nagging, or emotions. But you don't have to tone down your expectations. It's one thing to work to better your disciplinary style. It's quite another to abandon your discipline altogether.

Level five: The most deeply destructive level. The message is that you should measure your parenting by others' parenting. Nowadays, that's a sure path to raising a child quite unlike what you had hoped for. If the majority of parents' standards are slipping, and I believe so, then it is foolish to take the majority as a guide. If all the other parents jump into the lake, are you going to jump in, too?

I know what you're thinking. How did Dr. Ray get all those levels of interpretation from just a couple of statements? Remember, I'm a shrink. I'm practiced at overanalyzing. And I'm a parent. I'm practiced at overreacting.

The Right to Privacy

Dear Dr. Ray,

Do you think children have a right to privacy concerning their room and personal belongings?

An Appeal

The right to privacy. It may make for good constitutional debates, but it makes for real bad parenting.

A mother called my radio show upset that while cleaning her teenage daughter's room she had come across a letter describing her daughter's sexual behavior with her boyfriend. Part of Mom's distress was guilt over having "snooped," however unintentionally, and the fear of confronting her daughter, whom she knew would immediately hammer her with "You have no right to look through my things." (As an aside, if such were a daughter's first response, rather than embarrassment, guilt, or some display of conscience, then she would be telling Mom much about her view of sexual conduct. But back to the story.) The overall tone of the call was Mom's struggling more with her own psychological correctness than with her daughter's moral correctness.

A child's right to privacy is one more of many modern expert concoctions about child rearing. It is one that has taken a heavy toll on vigilant parenting. I can't fathom past generations wondering where their right to oversee their child's upbringing in their own home ended—at what point they were no longer allowed to be aware of their children's potentially harmful desires and actions.

The right to privacy. It may make for good constitutional debates, but it makes for real bad parenting.

At about age eleven, a friend's daughter, Sarah, created a personal diary in which she detailed and rehearsed her daily upsets and frustrations. My friend and his wife discovered it, talked with Sarah, and ended the diary.

Their reason? Sarah was not helping herself to deal better with the troubles of adolescence. She was emotionally dwelling on perceived injustices, with no adult feedback to counter her reiterating complaints. Private or not, the diary went out of print, as my friend and his wife judged that was the best (or maybe the least bad) of their parenting prerogatives.

Making bad decisions is nearly inescapable for humans, even the most mature of us. When those humans are only partly mature, as is even the most mature child, the odds of moving down self-harmful paths go up dramatically. So God gave children gatekeepers—parents—who are wiser (usually) and can help steer them away from bad paths, or close those paths altogether. If those gatekeepers surrender some of their God-given duty to guide and protect because of some trendy, silly, "democratic" notion of family, who is left to guard the children? The children are not capable of guarding themselves.

Of course, most parents don't do a mattress-by-mattress search of their kids' belongings in the absence of any evidence of trouble whatsoever. I'm not advocating such. What I am advocating is that children must know from Day One—at whatever age you decide that day falls—you will act resolutely at any time in any way to head off any trouble at first sniff of it.

The "right to privacy" has an honorable sound to it. It seems so respectful of a child's emotional boundaries. Yet it is dramatically superseded by another right: the right to safety. Far over and above any need to have secrets is the need to be protected from the results of those secrets. A parent's foremost duty is to guide a child to adulthood in good moral shape. Where that duty collides with a child's wants, the parent must win, for the sake of *all* the child's rights.

Forced Contact

Dear Dr. Ray,

My thirteen- and fourteen-year-olds, who used to love to be with my husband and me, are more and more reluctant to go anywhere with us. They always seem to have something "better" to do. Should we force the issue?

A Twosome Again

Ah, sweet parental revenge. During the first nine or ten years of life, in public the kids embarrass us. After that, we embarrass them. "Ah, c'mon, Dad, don't wear the shirt with the feathers again; Mom, please don't wave to me when other people are looking; just drop me off here. I'll walk the last couple miles."

The great adolescent aversion to being with us dorky grown-ups is as much cultural as developmental, if not more so.

Listening to grandparents and other older adults, I've come to believe that the great adolescent aversion to being with us dorky grown-ups is as much cultural as developmental, if not more so. In the not-so-distant past, double-digit age was not so routinely a predictor of resistance to public parental contact. Only as life for kids has become more frenetic and entertaining has the competition for what used to be family time exploded.

Why should Freeman want to go out to eat with his mother—a high-level treat a few generations back—when he can opt for home, call friends, surf the TV, play computer games, and then get picked up by Harley, who has a bigger TV, 3-D video games, and a cute sister who also stayed home to avoid being with her parents? In short, it's not always that your kids aren't pulled to be with you; it's that the pull to be elsewhere is much stronger. As the entertainment options expand with age, and nowadays they do so exponentially, their former top ten pick—being with Mom and Pop—drops to #47.

Many experts solemnly intone: It is normal and healthy for adolescents progressively to separate from adults and to assert their desires in the development of independence, or some such psycho-verbiage. I'll bet their kids don't want to be with them, either.

Certainly some separating is natural. But how is it that we have come to label wanting to spend little time with parents as somehow "healthy," psychologically speaking? Further, just because something is normal doesn't mean it's welcome or even always good. It also doesn't mean you have to stand back passively and let it dictate family life.

But so what if Freeman would rather be elsewhere than with you? What would you gain by forcing him to attend his little sister's Christmas play, or to visit elderly Aunt Agatha, the lady who always cries when she sees how big he's getting and who wants to hug and kiss him goodbye and give him a dollar? How much trauma can he take?

The answer depends on what you want to teach. If you don't mind that Freeman always chooses adolescent freedom over family, then let him pursue his pursuits. Someday he'll probably pass through this phase, although in the meantime don't listen to the song "Cat's in the Cradle"; it could make you nervous.

On the other hand, if you want to teach Freeman that, like it or not, some things are more important than entertaining yourself, then at times you do need to insist that he go your way instead of his. Gee, is it hard to figure out which direction I lean? You don't have to be a shrink to read between these lines.

Well, you might say, we do spend time together at home. True, but if you're like most families, even home time is at a premium. Why give teens the authority to decide to reduce further what little family time you already have? More important, not all lessons in character are taught at home. A visit to Aunt Agatha's, however boring in modern society's measure, can teach manners, sacrifice, respect for elders, and compassion.

Is all this to suggest that you hog-tie your kids and drag them kicking and screaming everywhere you go? Would you even want to do that to yourselves? I don't think so. I do think, however, that you need to judge each time together on its merits, and not on whether your kids want it.

Believe it or not, sometimes good times occur because parents insist on it. Once past their initial resistance, the kids find this isn't all so bad, assuming of course you change that shirt and don't do anything too uncool, like snort when you laugh. And even if your children don't cooperate now, chances are they'll see it differently some day. Many young adults have told me how grateful they are for those times of forced family contact, as forever memories were made.

There's an unexpected bonus to one-sided togetherness. The kids will be so ecstatic whenever they don't have to be with you, they'll probably do just about anything to earn freedom—even be nice to you in public.

Date and Age

Dear Dr. Ray,

My oldest daughter is fifteen. Most of her friends are beginning to date or have been dating. In general, when do you think is a good age to allow children to date?

Aging Fast

When they're married. And only with their spouse. Obviously, dating age depends upon all kinds of factors, and varies from child to child, even within the same family. But here are some general guidelines from my experience.

1. Most kids are dating way too early.
2. Never consider the cultural "average age" when making your decision.
3. Start slow and supervised.
4. When in doubt, hold off.
5. Nothing at all is to be gained by premature, opposite-sex involvement through dating, or for that matter, through the phone, dances, parties, or games.

This said, life truth #204 states that if you act differently from the way the majority does, you will be misunderstood by most. Let's suppose that you've decided to begin dating discussions when your daughter turns sixteen. Now back in the old days—the early 1980s—you met resistance for such a decision mainly from the children. Parents used to expect instinctively to be challenged by their kids, especially in judgments of how fast one should grow up.

What is quite different these days is that you are almost as likely to be questioned by your peers:

"These are different times. This is not when you and I were growing up. These kids grow up so much faster nowadays. You can't protect them forever. You can't wrap a moral bubble around them; they have to deal with life. If you make kids too different, they'll feel like weirdos who don't fit in. Then they'll get resentful and rebellious.

"I had a friend in California whose neighbor's boss had a son whose cousin's best friend wasn't allowed to date until he was seventeen, and I'll tell you what. He turned his back on everything his parents tried to teach him. When he got to college, he ran like a wild animal."

Life truth #204 states that if you act differently from the way the majority does, you will be misunderstood by most.

Yes, people have a penchant for arguing by exception. But let me share with you a rule. A recent survey suggested that if a child has a first date between the ages of eleven and thirteen, he or she has a 90 percent probability of being sexually active during senior year in high school. First date at age fourteen leads to a 50 percent chance; first date at age sixteen, 20 percent chance.

What chance would you prefer? What chance is much of society taking?

Key factors to consider in granting any type of dating freedom would be the child's moral maturity, independence of thought, history of conduct in other social settings, strength of will, social judgment, choice of friends, responsibility toward schoolwork, and respect for authority. I figure if I make the list long enough, my kids won't be eligible to date until they move out.

Once you are confident your son or daughter has met these standards, sit them down, let them know how much you admire who they are and who they're becoming. Then tell them, "Just three more years, and you can date."

Just kidding. Sort of.

Preaching More Than You Practice

Dear Dr. Ray,

Is it fair for me to expect conduct from my children that I don't always exhibit myself? I don't want to be a "do as I say, not as I do" parent.

Not Like Me

"Do as I say, not as I do" is part of every parenthood. In fact, it's a healthy part. What conscientious mother or father doesn't want a child to reach higher than they—in morals, character, and maturity? If you couldn't raise good kids with some of this style, children could never be better than their parents. We would be the upper limit of what our children could become. Now that's a scary thought, isn't it?

"Do as I do" is the ideal. It's something to strive for, and certainly it is the more durable form of parenting. It presents a child with a model to watch as well as guidelines to follow. Everybody—big and little—is expected to reach for the same standards.

Here's the catch. And it's the same catch that affects all our best intentions: our inescapable human weakness. We simply cannot think, feel, and act in every way we try to teach our kids. We're severely hampered by our human frailties.

If we linked expectations for our children to our own habits, waiting to discipline until we ourselves were well disciplined, would we ever discipline? If you smoke, do you want your

> **"Do as I say, not as I do" is part of every parenthood. In fact, it's a healthy part.**

twelve-year-old to smoke? Because your temper sometimes controls you, will you allow your son's temper free expression? Because your mouth sometimes has a mind of its own, does that make your son's disrespect permissible? Because you're nowhere near the person you want to be, will you deny yourself the responsibility to teach your daughter to be her best?

One advantage—maybe it's a disadvantage—of being a grown-up is that in much day-to-day behavior, we have to discipline ourselves. No one else can or will do it. If they could, I'd venture to say our conduct would be of a higher caliber. It is the loving duty of a parent, however, to provide the discipline that the child lacks, even though we ourselves sometimes lack self-discipline.

A mother complained to me that her eleven-year-old son was twenty pounds overweight, watched three to four hours of television per day, and showed little initiative with his schoolwork. When I asked her why she'd allowed all this to go on, she replied she felt guilty correcting him because she herself was overweight, watched too much TV, and struggled with self-initiative. No doubt, he was in part imitating her, but her habits were decades old, while his had been developing only a few years.

For his sake, she needed to use her parental will to force him in other directions even though her personal will was weak. I asked her one simple question: Do you want your son to have every bad habit you do? Of course, she said no. Then, I advised, make him move in different directions. Who knows? Maybe he'll become the role model for her.

Will kids fight being forced to live in ways we ourselves don't? Absolutely. Kids instantly zero in on any perceived inequity, even if it's for their own good. "Fine, I'll hang up my underwear, but when I'm grown up and have my own house, I'm never going to hang up my underwear, and I'm going to make you hang up yours before you ever come in the house."

As a rule, the closer you get to the "do as I do" style, the less friction you'll encounter from your children when you enforce the standards. They may still resist; after all, they won't behave maturely just because you do. But at the least, they can't fire the double standard accusation at you—not legitimately, anyway.

There's a bright side to seeing the discrepancy between how we act and how we expect our kids to act. It forces us to look harder at ourselves and stretch higher than we otherwise might. Everybody wins.

One Last Time

Repetition for emphasis. A good learning philosophy, except when it comes to wordy discipline. At the risk of nagging at you, one last time let's emphasize several core truths about good discipline.

1. *Discipline is love in action.* It is teaching at the most gentle hands a child will ever experience—a loving parent's. Discipline now, and the world won't have to discipline later.

2. *Good discipline is grounded in good sense.* It always has been. It always will be. "New and improved" parenting theories are new, but aren't always improved, and sometimes are much worse than time-tested methods.

3. *Good parents make mistakes, lots of them, and learn from them.* Disciplining in fear of mistakes only erodes self-confidence. And confidence is crucial to taking the hard-but-best stands.

4. *Strong discipline isn't complicated.* It's founded upon a few basics and the will to persevere with them. Discipline is easy, if you're willing to work hard at it.

5. *Discipline is action, not talk.* Discipline with consequences, and you'll discipline less. Discipline with mere words, and you'll discipline more. Action discipline leads to calmer and quieter discipline. Wordy discipline leads to louder and meaner discipline.

6. *All discipline interacts with a one-of-a-kind object: a child.* Some kids require one tenth of the average amount of discipline; some kids, ten times the average. Regardless, good parenting is parenting up to the very level required. Do what it takes, for as long as it takes. Your child deserves no less.

7. *Kids are wired to misbehave.* It's who they are. The concern is not so much that a child misbehaves. The concern is all the problems that come if the parent isn't willing to discipline. Expect misconduct, for years. Expect to discipline, for years. Time will reward you and your children.

8. *Humans resist discipline—some a little, some a lot.* Children are just better at resisting discipline than most. It's a fact of human nature that we often fight what is good for us. Resist your children's resistance. As they mature, they'll better understand and accept.

9. *Good parents are misunderstood.* Really good parents are really misunderstood. No longer is it only the children who question and accuse parents. Now it is other adults, who should know better. Strong parents face much opposition, not because they're wrong, but because they're right.

So stand strong. Reality always wins, and it is on your side.

DR. RAY GUARENDI is available for speaking engagements. To contact him, please call (330) 966-8019, or visit his website at **www.DrRay.com.**

To listen to Dr. Ray on his nationally syndicated radio program, *The Doctor Is In,* please check his website for an affiliate in your area. If you have no local affiliate, you can listen live at www.DrRay.com. To contact the program, call the number listed on the website during the program's hours of airing.